How to Be a Party Girl

Pat Montandon

How to Be a Party Girl

McGraw-Hill Book Company · New York · Toronto

Acknowledgment is made to Rudolf E. Noble, M.D., Ph.D., for permission to reprint "The Thinking Girl's Diet" which appears on pages 98–99.

To San Francisco, my constant source of inspiration

CONTENTS

CONTENTS

How to Be a Party Girl

CHAPTER ONE

Party of the First Part

Time: early evening. Weather: chilly clear, San Francisco at its finest. Dark blue sky, a sliver of new moon, a splash of stars, a wink of neon here and there. Clanging of cable-car bells. Laughter, perfume, packages, flowers, hurrying feet. A special kind of electricity in the air. It's that time of day again—my time of day—party time.

The cable car thunks to a halt at the corner of Hyde and Lombard. Off tumbles a bumper crop of working girls, homeward bound, including me. A good many of the faces are familiar by now. We stop at the curb for a minute, exchange weary grins, and then, at a break in the traffic, scatter.

Click, click, click. Now it's just me, clambering down the crazy-curlicue block of Lombard, "the crookedest street in the world." Then, when I've made it to the bottom of the hill, a deep breath, and up what always seem to be the steepest house-steps in the world. Two and a half flights, and will somebody please remind me to give these shoes to a girl with feet a couple of sizes smaller? Vanity,

vanity. Actually, it wasn't vanity at all, though—it was a sale at I. Magnin that got me this time.

Well, grab your mail, pick up that newspaper and what have you done with your key? No kidding, it's really there, right in your purse for a change? O.K. key, let's go.

And here's my place—white rug, white curtains, red roses, splashy paintings, white sofa, white cat curled on the sofa. Hi, Fluff. Shall we close the curtains? Let's not, for a minute. Look at that view! San Francisco Bay—the Bridge—the lights on the hills of Berkeley across the way—I'll never get used to it. Move over, Fluffcat, this gal you're living with didn't have time to lie around preening all day, like you. And now it's after six. The man who sent the roses is on his way—or else, he's hunting around in *his* pockets, for the key to his Rolls Royce. In forty-five minutes, I've got to be ready for a cocktail party, *La Bohème*, and Trader Vic's. Off with the shoes, on with the "Clean and Clear"—time for Operation Preparation.

The problem at the moment is the strap-marks from the bra I was wearing all day. My evening dresses are all cut down to you-know-where, and I have exactly forty-two minutes to decide what I am going to do about it. Let's make a memo on that right now, since this is going to be a book full of Handy Hints for Party Girls, O.K.? *Always run around the house naked for several hours before going to the opera.*

So here I am, fresh out of the shower five minutes later, and before I put on my new mink eyelashes I guess it's time to introduce myself. I'm Pat Montandon. They say I'm San Francisco's number one Party Girl. Well, I am a girl who loves to give fabulous parties—and loves to go to them too. If you've ever been in San Francisco (and if you

2

found time, while you were here, to read a newspaper) you've probably read about me. Maybe you've seen my picture too, in the papers and in the fashion magazines. I've received a lot of attention, and frankly, I love every bit of it. Parties are fun, and they're creative, too. Indirectly, entertaining has brought me my livelihood: in television, in the fashion business, modeling, advising on parties, on grooming and beauty, dozens of free-lance jobs in the glamour field. All this, and I'm only doing what I like to do anyway.

I'm not a Party Girl in the old-fashioned sense. I don't pop out of cakes at smokers, and I don't, as a general rule, dance on table tops. Come to think of it, I've never danced on a table top in my life. Maybe I've been missing something.

Well, here I am running around like crazy—don't worry, I'm almost ready, I've got my eyelashes and my perfume on now—and still I'll never believe all that has happened to me. You see, five years ago, when I first came to San Francisco, I was *the girl no one knew*. Have I mentioned that I am a preacher's daughter? Would you believe *two* ministers? My mother was an ordained minister also. I was born in a little place called Merkle, Texas. Get out your magnifying glass—you'll be sure not to find it on the map.

Nobody in Merkle, Texas, expected that little Patsy Lou Montandon would be famous some day as a hostess in San Francisco society. No one in Waurika, Oklahoma (population 2,000), where I grew up dreamed of any such thing either. Least of all me. It's a long way from the make-believe parties I used to give in my backyard as a six-year-old kid in Oklahoma, to the Carnaby Street bash I threw for two hundred Mod-costumed guests in San Francisco.

3

And it's a long, long way from the Waurika church social which was my Very Big Moment as a child to the soirée I arranged at Lake Tahoe for Frank Sinatra.

Or is it really such a long way? I'll let you in on a little something right now, which may surprise my swinging pals in San Francisco. Sure, I love it when they call me "Queen of the Jet Set" and praise me for all my great and original talents as a hostess. But the truth is, my success is solidly based on the old-fashioned brand of hospitality we learn young in the small country towns of the Southwest. Those church socials, for example. Each "covered dish" lovingly concocted by the hands of friends and neighbors —each posy on the table an offering from someone's garden. Everybody really glad to see everybody else. Nothing more exciting to drink, of course, than soda pop: a little different from the typical San Francisco party, where guests average seven jolts of firewater apiece by the end of the evening. And yet, we all had a blast, on 100-proof sarsaparilla, and ginger ale on the rocks. Without a doubt, my staunch old pals in Waurika taught me the most important thing I will ever learn about entertaining: the art of party-giving is essentially the art of giving. It's the art of caring, the art of wanting to please. Basically, it's a matter of really liking people.

A while ago, I went back home for a high school reunion—and they really do it up right in Waurika. The town was booming, crammed with five hundred ex-students who'd found their way back for the celebration, everything jumping with excitement as if someone had struck oil overnight. There were dances and picnics, and bands playing foot-stomping music. All my old friends gathered around me. "What's it like, Patsy Lou, to give a party for Frank Sinatra?" they asked. "How does it feel,

4

seeing a whole society page about it in the paper when you give a party? Have you turned into a rich society girl?" As they all knew, there had been no headlines when I graduated from high school, and if my family had given me a debut it probably would have been out back in the henhouse.

Well, I assured them that Henry Ford II hadn't adopted me, and told them quite truthfully that entertaining celebrities is no different from giving a party for people in Waurika or anywhere else. I had worried, as a matter of fact, about going home. Would I be stared at, and compared with the pictures in my press notices? Would I be scorned for my new big-city accent, not to mention the mink eyelashes?

Eyelashes! Here I am sitting around in my little pink bra-straps. What time is it, anyway? It's late. Oh well, *La Bohème*, here I come. I was going to tell you all my great, original secrets about getting dressed fast for a party. I swear, I'll write an entire chapter on the subject, first thing tomorrow morning.

Well, it was fun. One thing about a Rolls, the engine always works. And that's my kind of economy. Where was I? Oh yes, I was back in Waurika with everybody staring at my eyelashes. Except that they didn't. I was given such a welcome I'll never forget it. I arrived on the last remaining passenger car of a train that had been endless, when we left the Coast; if only I'd known, I would have decorated the whole thing with bunting and flown my personal flag. Well, no need. I was received with cheers and half smothered with hugs as soon as I stepped off the train. Everybody wanted to know all about my new life in San Francisco. I don't know why I'd worried about my accent—it

5

was gone, as soon as I opened my mouth, and all those chic clothes of mine were well dusted with red Oklahoma soil within half an hour or so. Before long I had my shoes off, and I was stomping to that back-country music with the best of them.

Remember, when you entertain celebrities, the more renowned you are the more you are apt to treasure a small-town background. You need to go back, and reassure yourself about that world of spontaneous living—spontaneous generosity. No press agents, just people who really love you. Celebrities are just like everybody else, only more so.

"Tell us about Frank Sinatra," said everyone, so I told them about that evening in Tahoe. Frank was a delightful guest—when he finally arrived. I was manager of the Joseph Magnin shop at Cal-Neva, a club on the Nevada side of Lake Tahoe, at the time. I had asked Frank to come to the little house I had rented nearby, and had assembled a group of friends who wanted to meet him. We waited and we waited. A San Francisco doctor's wife finally broke out in hives from sheer excitement. Luckily, her husband had brought along his medical kit, and he was busy giving her a shot when finally the telephone rang.

"Patty baby, I'm on my way, but I'm lost," said Mr. Sinatra. I gave him further directions, and he left the startled summer visitor whose telephone he had borrowed. The story was that she wouldn't let anyone else touch that phone for the rest of the summer. Everybody loves you, see, Frank baby?

Everybody but Kaiser, that is. Kaiser was an enormous Great Dane, my chaperon that summer, and guardian in the wilds. He was a marvelous dog. I had a beau who used to write letters to him, in fact. Just before the Sinatra

6

party a letter came (I still have it) saying, "See here, Kaiser, you keep your bargain about those others guys who will show up there. You know what to do, Kaiser—not up to the elbow, just a damn good chunk out of the forearm or the leg will suffice."

Well, you know, I really think that dog could read. Frank came swinging up the path all smiles, and before I could utter a word he reached out to pat the dog. "They love me," he told me reassuringly just as Kaiser leaned over and bit his wrist.

My friends in Waurika thought that was pretty funny, and I had to admit it was, but poor Frank! And what a way for me to demonstrate my marvelous skills as a hostess! Amazingly enough, it turned out to be a wonderful evening. No stitches, no tourniquets—and whatever trauma Mr. Sinatra may have suffered, he was so good-natured about it that I'll be grateful to him forever. He came into the house as jolly as could be, and made himself utterly charming to all my guests.

It's a little harder, of course, to keep smiling when the house burns down. That happened to me once too. Not in the middle of a party, but believe me, it was part of my Basic Training. Tragedy is like that. You learn from it, one way or another. Either you decide to cuddle up with yourself forever after, living scared (which is to say, not living at all), or you come out of it with all your flags flying. I decided a long time ago that I'd rather fly those flags than hide in a closet with a fistful of damp Kleenex. I was lucky—I found out when I was in real trouble just how wonderful people can be.

I was fourteen years old when my dad died, leaving Mother with eight children, nearly destitute. Then the house burned down. I was standing in the kitchen, cooking dinner for my little brother. We were the only ones home; Mother had been called away to care for a sick relative. Suddenly the stove exploded. We escaped just in time to stand in the yard and watch everything we had left in the world go up in flames. I was wearing a bathrobe, and my brother had a pair of jeans. That was it.

I was too shocked even to cry. All I could think of was my poor mother, coming home that night on the train. She had worked so hard for us. What could I say to her—how could I ever tell her?

Our friends in the town gathered around us, brought us clothes, and went in a large group to the station with us. I will never forget my mother's face as she saw us standing there. She knew that something terrible had happened, and yet her look said, before she could reach out her arms to me, No matter what, I love you. As I tried to stammer out the news, the neighbors said to her, "Don't you worry about anything. We're going to take care of you."

Take care of us they did, we moved in with those wonderful neighbors of ours. And as for my mother, a little thing like the loss of everything she owned wasn't going to dim her spirit. She took what funds we had, $400 in insurance, and managed to buy a lovely old farmhouse in the country for $200, and had the house moved to a lot in town which she bought with our last remaining pennies. Then she went back to work, taking care of her parish. Soon we noticed that the people of the church were all abuzz with excitement: a shower was being planned for us. I can hardly begin to tell you what that shower was like. They gave us everything, from a stove down to spoons and forks, and what are known in the Southwest as "cup towels" (dish towels, to the uninitiated). They even gave us their own hand-embroidered family linens. But the sweetest gift of all was the last one announced at the shower.

Along with everything else in the fire I had lost my most prized graduation present, a really nice blue chiffon blouse. I loved pretty clothes then as much as I do now, and I had grieved secretly for that little touch of glamour, even while we were all wondering how we were going to eat.

The ladies of the church stood up and one said, beaming at me, "Sister Montandon and Miss Patsy Lou, we have one final gift." They handed me a package, all done up with ribbon curls. I opened it, and there was an exact duplicate of my beloved blue chiffon blouse!

Years later, when I arrived in San Francisco, alone and without a job or a home to welcome me, I brought with me the memory of that day in faraway Waurika. The old blue blouse went to the rag pile long ago, but I will not forget what it stood for.

I came to this city, like so many other young people, looking for a fresh start in life after a time of struggle and disappointment. San Francisco—the Golden City, the Last Frontier. I was unhappy, divorced, and broke, but filled with hope, somehow, that here I would find myself and make a new beginning. San Francisco is beautiful—I think it's the most beautiful city in the world. But all cities are lonely when you first arrive and you don't know anyone. I wondered, that first night, crossing the Bridge, seeing the lights of the city for the first time—what would happen to me? Would I find a place to live—would I find a job? And if I did, would I be just another working girl, lost in the crowd, going home nights to a dingy little room—a

9

hot plate, peanut butter and sardines—yesterday's stockings hanging in the shower? I wanted something better than that.

San Francisco is a tough city for outsiders, I'd heard. The social sets were closed to newcomers, especially single girls who didn't come armed with letters of introduction from classmates at Vassar or from Mummy's old pals at Farmington. This girl's mummy didn't go to Farmington, that's for sure. And I got my college education waiting on tables at the Four Star Café, Waurika, Oklahoma.

As I sat there, feeling very glum, in the bus that was bringing me into town, a flashy sports car zipped by below me, with a handsome young man at the wheel and a spectacular blonde at his side, her blue-green scarf fluttering behind her in the wind. Envy is a sin, you know. And I sinned like mad, watching those two speed by, all casual and carefree, while I crouched with my feet on my suitcase trying not to bite my fingernails.

Well, I don't have to envy anyone any more, and I'm not boasting, I'm just stating a fact. I've worked hard for my success, and I'm proud of it. The whole point of this book is, anyone can do it. It's not a matter of luck, it's a matter of determination and skill.

My first years here were spent learning the ropes of the fashion business, at Saks and Joseph Magnin, and getting myself established as a model. Everywhere I went I looked around me, found people that I liked, and gradually built up a little group of good friends. I gave a few small parties—very modest at first, and simple as could be.

Then, suddenly it happened, and my life changed almost overnight. It was an idea for a party that did it. I was off in Puerto Vallarta, on a typical travel-now-plead-later working girl's holiday. I'd been roaming the native mar-

10

kets there, feasting my eyes on all the wild fabrics and ceramics and the brilliant paper flowers. A scene popped into my mind: I'd give a Mexican Fiesta Party in San Francisco. It would be tremendous! I'd import everything, invite everyone—have Mexican food, Mexican music—the whole thing was obvious. Utterly crazy, of course, because I had no idea in the world how I was going to pay for it.

That's why I mailed the invitations the very next day from Mexico. Once you start worrying too much about money in this world your brains simply melt away. And I was having enough trouble staying alive in that Mexican heat wave. The fifty invitations I sent cost me all of $5, and they caused a sensation back in San Francisco. I had persuaded one of the maids at my hotel to write them in Spanish for me, and had borrowed some delightful little Mexican figures to decorate them, thanks to a dear friend who introduced me to Manuel Lepé, one of Mexico's foremost primitive painters. He was charmed with the idea for the party, and cut up his sample cards for me to use.

The party decorations were inexpensive too. I bought armfuls of those huge paper flowers—red, orange, and hot pink—and bolts of cheap cotton fabric in the same vibrant colors. Plenty of candles too, and as many Mexican pottery pieces as I could carry away.

Everyone was talking about "Pat's party" when I came home. Society editors had given it a big play, and one of my beaux was running around town collecting all the invitations he could find as souvenirs. I had asked some people I didn't know very well, but I had a great pile of acceptances waiting for me, many of them in Spanish. Obviously I had hit on something which intrigued people, and I was a success before the party started.

And what a party it was! I hung the lengths of fabric in great swags from my balcony, and put candles in the pottery pieces all the way up the front steps. Inside, my rooms were transformed, with most of the furniture put away, and more fabrics swagged around here and there, with huge bouquets of paper flowers. I discovered a marvelous Mexican trio that played the boisterous songs of their homeland all evening for a very reasonable fee and a negligible amount of tequila. And if you had seen and tasted the buffet you wouldn't have known that I couldn't afford a caterer. The society editors never guessed. A gifted friend had helped me prepare the tortillas, the enchiladas, the filet of beef, smoked salmon and caviar soufflé.

The next morning the telephone nearly rang itself off the hook with congratulations. The newspapers reported the most "original" and "exotic" party of the season. People began asking my advice about parties of their own, and of course I was suddenly in demand everywhere as a guest. I was working in a good-enough junior executive job at the time, but things began to happen after my "fiesta," and now, several years later, I have a full-time career freelancing in my chosen field.

Sometimes it is parties. Right now, for instance, I am helping three bachelors plan a Great Lovers Party. People are supposed to come as historical personages noted for this sort of thing, or famous lovers of the present day. It's great fun—all very elaborate—and it should result in some dandy combinations before the evening is over.

Glamour is part of the deal too, so I have been hired to supervise grooming classes for employees of World Airways and of two major banks, the Bank of America, and the United California Bank. I am fashion consultant for Hart, Schaffner and Marx, and fashion editor for *Curtain*

Call, a theatre magazine. Recently I organized a series of seminars in San Francisco on glamour and entertaining, with fellow experts to help me cover the field. I've appeared on TV a good deal as a special guest, and now appear each weekday on ABC-TV, Channel 7, San Francisco, as hostess for a regular morning program.

My parties have brought me all this, and above all they have brought me people, people, people. Complete strangers come up and say, "Hi, Pat, how are you?" Sometimes people I don't even know ask to come to my parties. One man recently offered to bar-tend free for me if I would just send him an invitation! *Playboy* magazine telephoned and asked me to pose for their center foldout, but I declined with thanks. Experts in the entertainment field tell me there's such a thing as overexposure, and I certainly wouldn't want to be a bore.

A lot of people want to know whether or not I have a press agent. Well, I don't, and I never wanted one. I don't like the idea of drumming up interest. Some people say to me, "Pat, I just can't figure you out. You're such a bundle of contradictions." Well, it's very simple, really. I'm a practical-minded, plain-spoken, rather prim girl—who just happens to love doing flamboyant things.

I put in longer hours very often now than I did as a junior executive, but I couldn't care less. It doesn't matter, when you are doing what you enjoy. As for pay, I haven't become rich, but I do keep a regular budget for my parties, just as other girls might save for a Jaguar or a Paris suit. The money I've spent in entertaining has come back to me many times over in commissions, new job contacts —and in the things that are far beyond price: friends, ideas, glamour and beauty in my life, and plenty of just plain fun.

13

If you're on your own and new in town, any town, then this book is especially for you. But I'm going to include information about all kinds of parties for all kinds of people before I'm through. If you're going to give first-rate parties you've got to know all you can, about every one of the ingredients. So we'll discuss them all, step by step—guests (and how to find them, if you're new at the game), basic techniques of being a good hostess, different kinds of parties that are fun to give, party themes, food, liquor, men, party helpers of all kinds, and how to pay the piper his due.

Remember, though, if you're female you've got half the battle won already, just because the essential ingredient of any party you give is you. As a woman you were born to please, and you were born creative. It was a smart cave man, all right, who discovered fire and figured out that artichokes are good to eat. I'm sure nothing of the sort would have occurred to me. But I'll bet it was his wife who got the candles on the table and invented hollandaise sauce. Or if it wasn't his wife he married her the next day.

There's no limit to the imagination you can use planning your own parties, once you know some of the basic principles. Help yourself to all the tips you need, but when you have finished this book don't forget, you learn best by doing. So go ahead, give a party of your own. Everybody into the punchbowl except the kid with the dirty sneakers!

CHAPTER TWO

Where Is Everybody?

The first party I ever gave was a hen party. That is to say, it was for hens. I was seven years old at the time, and since we were living on a farm several miles from Waurika my social circle consisted of a bunch of dumb clucks.

I set up an egg crate, covered it with an old flour sack, and concocted a lavish buffet which included Koolaid in jelly glasses and bread-butter-and-sugar sandwiches. Hedy and Carole were my guests of honor: two of the finest, plumpest hens, who had become my special pets. I'd found their names in the magazines my brother kept hidden in the hayloft. Errol the rooster was locked up in the chickenyard for the occasion, poor creature. . . . I had a lot to learn yet as a hostess in those days.

Needless to say, the hen party laid an egg. But that's another story. The problem at hand is: you're new in town and you want to give a party, but what are you going to do for guests? Presumably, you aren't keeping chickens in your flat.

Once you've worked your way up to becoming a first-rate hostess, you will have a large group of friends and acquaintances to choose from, according to what kind of a party you have in mind. If you are the methodical type you may have them listed in a convenient file, along with their addresses, telephone numbers, and other information. The filing cabinet of an experienced Party Girl is one of her most precious possessions.

But where are you going to find these people when you need them most—at the beginning, when you're alone and you don't like it? A great many people have to cope with this sort of situation. Ours is a mobile age, and few of us remain in the town or city where we were born. Above all, don't make the mistake of sitting around feeling sorry for yourself. That takes time, and makes for circles under the eyes. Go to work instead, and make a beginning for yourself by being friendly and hospitable to the people you meet on the job.

Once, when I first arrived in San Francisco, I invited a girl from my office for dinner, not because I thought she was the greatest person in the world but because she was someone whose name I knew at least. Then too, I was a little curious about the attractive man I'd noticed picking her up occasionally after work. Well, he turned out to be her husband. But there were consolations. Two of his former college friends had just arrived in the city and wanted to meet people. So I was invited back to the home of the young married couple, and we were introduced. Other people were present—a group that was mostly new to me—and I made a good many new friends that evening.

Make a list of all the people you speak to in the course of one week—people interesting enough, potentially at least, to be invited to a party. You'll be surprised, I promise you, at the length of that list—unless you're walking

16

around town with blinders on, and a mouthful of green persimmons. Well, get rid of the excess baggage. Somebody out there is waiting and hoping to meet a girl exactly like you.

Add to this list the names of all the people from your home town who happen to be in the area, and all the graduates from your school or college who have migrated to the city where you are. Chances are, your potential guest list at this point is already too large for you to manage easily.

Consider, then, enlisting a few helpers for a reunion of school friends or people from your home town. In many places cooperative parties are popular among members of the younger set. As far as I am concerned, B.Y.O.B. (Bring Your Own Bottle) parties are not acceptable, as they often dissolve into isolated drinking bouts. I prefer to be the hostess and make my own arrangements. If some nice man wanted to play host, and help me with the liquor bill, of course I wouldn't argue.

I know a girl named Marge who recruits party guests in an interesting way. She has it firmly fixed in her head that she is going to marry a banker some day, and so she invites as many of them to her parties as she can snag. She is convinced that bankers make good husbands—dignified, secure, stable, and they know how to balance a checkbook too. This is her technique for meeting them:

"I walk into a bank—any bank—very cool and calm, looking my best. Then I go up to some nice-looking young man I've spotted behind the counter, and I ask him if he will give me some help.

"'I just can't understand balance-plus (or something). Can you explain it to me?' So he explains, and then I tell him I am sorry I'm so stupid and I say I suppose his wife understands all about such things. This is the turning point. If they're married, they can't resist telling you how their wife is wonderful—or else she's hopeless—at numbers. So then you know."

If the coast is clear, Marge continues to pay little visits with further questions for the young man to answer. By the time they have had several consultations she feels it's quite proper for her to invite "her banker" to a party. "Some of them are shy, of course," she says, "and need more time. But one young man asked me for a date the second time I went back."

"What happens," I asked, "if the young man refuses your invitation?"

"Oh," replied Marge, "then I just take my money out and go to another bank. There are lots of banks."

It's true, new banks seem to be springing up all the time in the big cities. I don't know what significance this has in terms of the national economy, but a girl like Marge could make quite a project out of the situation.

Other girls I know are equally resourceful about meeting new people. My friend Ellen gave a Bring a Stranger Party which resulted in all sorts of interesting developments. At the time of her party she had built up a potential guest list of six single men and six single women. Ellen decided, why not go for double? So she asked each of her friends to bring a stranger of the opposite sex for cocktails. To make it challenging, she insisted that the "stranger" had to be unknown to the person issuing the invitation until the evening of the party.

The Scavenger Hunt was on. It was no problem for the men, but the girls felt a bit more timid about the situation. One girl drew a deep breath and invited a Frenchman she found in front of a bookstore, waiting for a taxi. He was *enchanté*. Another stopped at an art gallery on her way home, looked over the other visitors, and finally decided to ask the manager at closing time if he would like to accompany her to a small gathering of art enthusiasts. He too accepted with pleasure. The other girls played it safe and asked friends to provide them with "strangers"—all except Ellen herself. She of course had had something special in mind all along. A splendid-looking young bachelor had recently moved into her apartment house, and she now had a perfect excuse to march boldly upstairs and ring his doorbell. "We're having a Bring a Stranger Party. Will you be my stranger?" she asked. He accepted, and when last I heard they had both moved to Los Angeles.

A good many parties, some of them rather large, at that, have been dreamed up by single girls who have a certain male guest primarily in mind. A party is a useful piece of camouflage for the girl who doesn't wish it to be known, that she's in pursuit—and you can amuse yourself at the next party you go to, given by a bachelor girl, by trying to guess who may be the unsuspecting guest of honor. Better yet, you can try the ploy yourself. Don't restrict yourself to one dreamboat, though, unless you're absolutely sure he'll show up. Invite three or four of the men you'd like to know better—or make it an even dozen, and share the wealth with your office-mates. If you have too *many* men circling around you, any girl you know will be happy to help you with that little problem.

Even though you are single yourself, don't think only in terms of single people when you begin to build your personal guest list. Couples will be important in your life, and they can become invaluable friends and allies for life, especially if you can resist flirting with the husbands. It's a temptation, I know, and there are an awful lot of married

men who make it all too plain that they are "available"
—but don't be a dummy. If you are building a reputation
for yourself in a new city, and trying to find a permanent
place among friends who will respect you, the worst thing
you can do is create a lot of excitement among the married
men of the community. Concentrate instead on being
friendly to the wives and make it absolutely clear to them
that you are not interested in party games that take on the
shape of the well-known triangle. It's the wives who make
up the guest lists in most families, you know. And even if
they want to get rid of their husbands, they're not going
to appreciate any help from you.

A married woman can be a wonderful friend, if you can
endure her compulsive attempts at matchmaking! Be a
good sport, and don't discourage her. The next man she
drags forth from her husband's office may be just the one
you've been looking for. And if not, he may be a good
addition to your invitation list. A party is always better
with extra men. I learned that the very first time I enter-
tained. Poor Hedy and Carole were disconsolate, and as
for Errol, he never spoke to me again.

There are men, and then, of course, there are other
kinds of men. The problem of whether or not to invite
"gay boys" to your parties is one you ought to decide for
yourself. You may not have observed any in your home
town, but in the larger cities, especially on the East and
West Coasts, homosexuals are a part of the social scene.
Not lisping, mincing types, but perfectly presentable people who are often well-read, talented and amusing. Some
hostesses say that homosexuals are among the most charming, attentive and helpful guests you can invite to any
party, and I myself have many friends of this sort. I think
a woman who is sure of herself *as* a woman can afford to
20

associate with people who deviate from the norm. Follow your own feelings about it, of course, but remember, women need all kinds of men in their lives, men of all types, all ages, and varying interests. You are not going to fall in love with all of them—not unless you are off your rocker. You appreciate them, each in a different way, for a different reason.

Appreciate the women you meet too. Show your self-confidence by inviting a glamour girl or two to each of your parties. Let your guests enjoy the spice and glitter they add to the scene, and if they make you feel awkward by comparison at first, then get to know them better, and find out what you can learn from them. If you think of other women as your natural enemies they'll be sure to return the compliment. And that's sort of unnecessary, when you stop to think about it.

If you are artistically inclined you can arrange interesting parties by getting to know some of the younger artists in your city. They may not be starving in the traditional garret, but chances are they are starving for recognition. If your interest is genuine they are bound to appreciate it most gratefully. Don't patronize them, however, and don't invite friends to a showing of the artist's work unless this is made clear in the invitation. It's quite all right to give such a party. Guests are under no obligation to buy, but they should be notified in advance exactly what to expect.

By the same token don't invite singers, musicians or dancers to perform at your party without making the terms of payment quite clear in advance. And do not invite people well known to have such talents with the idea that they are there to entertain your guests. They may do so, of course, if they happen to be in the mood, but it is out of the question to make them feel obligated. One lady

I know made a terrible gaffe of this sort, and paid for it very dearly. The story is funny only because she could afford it, and because she should have known better to begin with. She invited a world-famous concert pianist to one of her soirées, and when he arrived he found a grand piano placed in the center of her very large drawing room, with little chairs all around, and all the assembled guests ready to sit down at the hostess' command and listen to him play. He was exhausted from his current concert tour, and had planned to remain at the party for only a few moments. Nevertheless he sat down at the piano without a word, played magnificently for two hours, rewarded the enthusiasm of his audience with several encores, and left his hostess with a polite bow and a gallant kiss upon the hand. The following morning, she received a bill for $2,000—exactly what she deserved.

Visiting celebrities are often available as guests in private homes when they are on tour. Just remember, they are your guests, and not there to perform. Their public relations may benefit from such invitations, and let's face it, hero worship is hard to turn down! Consider the possibility of building a party around such a person as guest of honor, and then contact his publicity agent to see if a date can be arranged. The theatre or hotel in question will generally put you in touch with the agent, whose business it is, after all, to see that his client meets the public—so you needn't feel apologetic. You might want to invite an entire group in this way—actors in town with a road company, a TV crew or movie group on location. Often you'll find them very enthusiastic and appreciative of the chance to come to a private home and meet people in a party situation. They like to eat and drink too—and one sure thing, the party is never dull.

In some towns and cities you can do a good deed for international relations while giving yourself and your guests a chance to meet people from other countries. This is certainly true in San Francisco, where we have many foreign consulates and a continuous parade of visitors from all over the world. Lovely women in saris or kimonos and magnificent young men in turbans are a commonplace sight at parties here—and yet such people never fail to fascinate other guests. They are delightful guests, interested in everyone they meet, and sincerely grateful for the hospitality they receive. I cannot recommend this sort of arrangement too highly to the girl who wants to give really interesting parties. And it isn't nearly as difficult to manage as you might think.

Agencies exist in most cities specifically for the purpose of helping foreign visitors with their social contacts. The International Hospitality House in San Francisco provides a clearing house for foreign visitors who want to meet Americans, or to go sightseeing, or to be taken into a typical American home. The Institute of International Education introduces many very fine foreign artists, writers, and other professionals to people in our country who share their interests and show a desire to entertain them. Don't hesitate to make use of these services.

A sure way to give a boring party is to invite a group of people who were all stamped out by the same cooky-cutter: same age, same background, same interests, same opinions. Don't do it! Mix types at your parties, and age groups, too. Older people are wonderful party guests—the ones with character and *joie de vivre*, of course—not the dreary souls who live in the past, resent the present, and fear the future. My own file of party guests includes many older men and women who are great fun on any occasion.

It's interesting too, I think, how they tend to influence the younger guests. Long-neglected qualities like chivalry, consideration for others, and appreciation suddenly spring to the fore. Manners become more elegant, timid souls blossom into wits, and the hostess herself is far more relaxed than usual, knowing that the party will be carried along smoothly by the superior poise and social experience of her older guests.

I don't know what I would have done without a grand old man I always call Stone Face. He was part of my life back in Waurika, and he still watches over me today. I was fifteen years old when I met Stone Face. He used to come into the café where I worked, every single day, order his meal, eat it, put a tip on the table, and depart without smiling or saying one friendly word. One day he said to me in his usual dour way, "I'll have an omelette." Well, this was a new one on me, but I wanted to be helpful, so I replied, "We don't have any omelettes; how about some scrambled eggs?"

He looked at me and for the first time I saw a smile. Then he threw back his head and laughed. I couldn't believe it. "You're laughing," I blurted out before I stopped to think, "and I didn't even know you could smile. I always call you Stone Face." He laughed harder than ever, and our little joke began a friendship which has lasted to the present day. I never know when the phone will ring and it will be a call from Stone Face in Waurika. "Are you all right, Patsy Lou?" he wants to know, and then I have to tell him all about my life in San Francisco. One day he thought I sounded a little depressed or something, so he got on a plane and came all the way to San Francisco. Granite-faced as ever, he arrived at the airport, taxied to my apartment, and climbed the steps to see if I

24

was *really* all right. He looked all around, asked me a hundred questions, and after chatting a bit about old times, and resting for a few hours at the St. Francis, got aboard another plane and went back to Waurika.

If you come from a small town you've known people like Stone Face all your life. It's hard to meet them in the city, and yet you know how much you need them. The social occasion is the city girl's substitute for the natural, everyday associations which are a part of small-town life. Make your parties work for you in this way. Build with them toward a new community of friends which will be valuable and nourishing. People you *don't* need on your list are the phonies and bores who have nothing to offer and wouldn't want to share it if they did. Watch out for men who merely use you and your parties as a way to get around where the girls are—and where the liquor is. Watch out, too, for girls who are your dearest friend when there are no men around, then unsheath their claws and turn into back-biting cats in a mixed group.

Get to know as much as you can about all prospective guests: what are their real interests, how do they tend to react in a group? Some people are great tête-à-tête, but if you ask them to parties sooner or later you are going to regret it. Telephone a mutual friend for advice on this, if necessary. Don't gossip—just inquire, then change the subject.

Now, are you ready to give a party? Start small, invite two or three people who really interest you, people you'd like to know better. Set the scene attractively for them. Nothing elaborate in the way of decorations, of course, for such a tiny party, but do something charming and unusual. Seashells, perhaps, and inexpensive green and blue glass balls as a centerpiece, instead of flowers. Pots of geraniums, maybe, standing by your front door as a special gesture of welcome. Please have candles in the living room, as well as your dining area! They make the women feel prettier, and the men more romantic. Besides, if you know you are going to entertain by candlelight you won't waste energy scrubbing the far corners of the room the day before the party. Prepare a meal that is well within your means—something completely simple and utterly delicious—serve it with a first-rate bottle of wine, and a minimum of fuss. Concentrate on looking pretty, feeling good, and enjoying yourself at your own party. Tell your guests how happy you are to have them there. They, in turn, will soon be telling you how grateful they are to have been invited, and meaning it wholeheartedly.

Now watch your social circle begin to expand. Once you have a fairly substantial list of potential guests you can be more and more selective as each occasion comes along. Feminine intuition, plus a little experience, will teach you quickly which people mix well with what others on your list. Making a party group is like mixing a superb salad or a perfect martini. You blend the personalities of your guests in proportions calculated quite consciously to please and delight. Practice makes perfect, but there is one rule which I've found particularly helpful: always provide your group with a suitable proportion of "listeners" to go with the "talkers."

A sympathetic "listener" is a boon to any hostess, but if many of your friends are the high-powered, articulate type this can be a crucial matter. One of my dinner parties turned into a disaster of major proportions because of the lack of sufficient audience. I had invited a fashion consultant, a television personality, the merchandise manager of a women's high-fashion store, an interior decorator, and

26

a certified public accountant. Most of them, as I well knew, were highly extroverted, rather aggressive people —fascinating to be with one at a time, but I don't know where my brains were the day I decided to invite them all together. I guess I must have been counting on that CPA.

Well, wouldn't you know it, the man turned out to be a champion long-distance talker on his own favorite subject, which happened to be, of all things, mushrooms. He brought a ten-pound specimen he'd grown himself to the party and insisted that I serve it with the cocktails. Everyone else wanted the floor at the time, of course, each for his own purposes. But Mr. Fungus-Fancier shouted them all down. They became annoyed, then furious. A lengthy argument ensued as to whether or not the horrible object ought to be cooked, and if so, how. I retreated with it into the kitchen, thinking to quiet things down, but in my absence our charming friend pressed his advantage further. The other guests were perspiring with frustration by the time we sat down to dinner, and by the time we reached the petits fours they were utterly glassy-eyed with despair.

There was nothing I could do. I tried, heaven knows, but nothing worked. We had to hear all about the gill, the stype, the velum, the mycelium, the et cetera; and we had to listen while he quoted every reference to mushrooms in the entire history of English literature. You'd be surprised how many there are. By the end of the evening I was ready to commit murder in the first degree, and I had four willing accomplices, I'm sure.

This particular guest was unpardonably rude, but a skillful raconteur with the gift of courtesy can be the making of a small party, if the hostess has provided him with listeners. I recall a nuclear physicist who kept a dinner

27

table spellbound as he discoursed about *his* hobby, which was cabinetmaking. The men appreciated his thorough knowledge of the craft, and the women, of course, were charmed by his enthusiasm for antique reproductions—a subject dear to the feminine heart. This gentleman turned his remarks first toward one guest, then to another, in a way that was so friendly and relaxed that we all found him utterly irresistible. And we were grateful, too, that a man in his position never once found it necessary to mention The Bomb.

It's hard for most men to keep their private lives separate from their occupations. And this causes special problems for the hostess who wants to help people forget their troubles and relax at party time. The fact is that many men count on parties to provide business and professional contacts which are important to their careers. At the club, over the bridge table, lunching at a restaurant, future transactions may be arranged or implied; and it is true that a considerable amount of America's business today takes place at private parties, which may have been arranged specifically for that purpose. For the single girl this is quite all right, because she has a choice in the matter. She can avoid social situations which don't appeal to her.

Wives of businessmen are stuck with it, however, and I know that some of them find it very trying indeed. As a married Party Girl, you have certain built-in advantages: greater security, of course, and a wider circle of acquaintances provided by your husband's business contacts. Maybe you'll find good friends for yourself this way. On the other hand, maybe you'll find yourself entertaining people you'd rather not have on your list. To put it plainly, maybe you'll find yourself sitting in your own living room, bored cross-eyed.

It's happened to the best of us. Think how Cleopatra must have felt when Antony brought a dull bunch of Roman generals home for dinner. Think how Josephine felt when Napoleon wanted her to entertain all those Corsican relatives of his! Tell yourself you're going to make Party Girl First Class by meeting this challenge with everything you've got.

The term "helpmate" isn't used much nowadays—it has an old-fashioned sound. But that's what you are. Make the house as pretty as you can, fix marvelous food, and then get yourself in a friendly sort of mood before the guests arrive.

Greet these unwanted guests with enthusiasm. You're not being phony, you're being a wife who cares about every part of her husband's life because she cares for *him*. Look after their needs with special care. Take another look at *them* while you're at it, too. Maybe the flashy husband who is so fond of telling off-color stories will quiet down under your expert guidance, and talk instead in a fascinating way about his wartime experiences, or his secret passion for gourmet cooking. Maybe the drab little wife trots downtown every Thursday night to teach classes in karate, or belly-dancing. A wise man once told me, "Find out what a person really loves in life and you'll have the key to understanding that person."

The situation could be a good deal worse than this, however. No belly-dancing, no karate, no gourmet cooking! As a dutiful wife you might find yourself entertaining people who quite obviously *care* about nothing at all. There are a certain number of them around and about, and I'm sorry to say that they do tend to turn up at this sort of dinner party.

Well, don't despair, even so. Play a game with yourself

instead: pretend you are putting on a "benefit" and carry it through as carefully as if you were selling tickets for your favorite charity. Enjoy the details of your own performance, by all means. Comfort yourself with the thought of how noble, helpful, and considerate you are being. Stiff upper lips look lousy on most women. *Enjoy* your virtue. You'll live longer and stay prettier.

Any opportunity to meet new people should be welcomed, on general principles, by the up-and-coming Party Girl. The more people you know, the better your parties will be. And your parties, in turn, will teach you more and more about people. Make them comfortable—draw them out—and look for surprises from the quiet types! I remember asking, quite doubtfully, a very mousy and nondescript young man to fill a place at one of my dinner parties. Eight o'clock came on the appointed evening, but no Mr. Willie G. I was about to give up on him, and change my entire seating plan, when suddenly he appeared on the scene. "Sorry to be late," he murmured, "but I was just indicted by the grand jury."

Some hostesses might have reached for the smelling salts, I suppose, but not me. I said, "Well, my dear, come right in and tell us all about it!" And little Willie was the hit of the evening.

CHAPTER THREE

Baker's Dozen: Dos and Don'ts for Hostess and Guests

The other day I came home from a modeling job in the middle of the morning wearing the marvelous tiger-print, full-length chiffon gown I'd posed in, and a blond "fall" that made me look as if I'd been growing my own hair for years. After waltzing around the house by myself for a while, I thought what a pity it was to waste all this! Why not give a party, right now.

It was a sparkling, sunny day, so I brought my yellow linen cloth and napkins out to the table in my little garden, and arranged a bouquet of fresh-picked daisies. A few phone calls summoned a dozen friends, and the beau of the moment was dispatched to Fisherman's Wharf for cracked crab and French bread. All I had to do was mix a green salad, put a couple of bottles of California wine in to chill, start the coffee perking—and luncheon was served.

We had a wonderful time—all the better, perhaps, because it was unexpected. The sound of our laughter floating up from the secluded garden and the sight of the hostess running up and downstairs in that exotic outfit must have convinced a good many of the passing tourists that they really ought to move to San Francisco.

It's fun to give impromptu parties, but if you're as busy as I am, doing everything *but* housework, it's wise to hold the phone a minute before collecting a large group of friends, and ask yourself a few solemn questions like: "Is this the day the plumber promised to come bail out the guest bathroom, or was that yesterday?" and "Is there anything in the house to eat except that old jar of capers, and half a dozen cans of Tuna-4-Cats?"

If you're the impulsive type, by all means keep a few instant-party menus pinned to the inside of your kitchen cupboard, with a list of ingredients which you check off every time you shop for food. If you keep, for example, a few cups of flour on hand at all times, and something to stuff crêpes with (a can of creamed turkey, or condensed cream-of-shrimp soup, with herbs and Madeira wine to jazz up the flavor), you've got the makings of an elegant little luncheon or supper party at a moment's notice. All you have to do is learn to make crêpes.

Every girl in this world should know how to dance beautifully, how to flirt successfully, how to make love divinely—and how to make crêpes. As for the latter, it isn't as difficult as you may think. What you do is, you go to a bookstore and buy yourself a copy of Julia Child's *Mastering the Art of French Cooking*. It's not cheap, but it's one of the best investments you will ever make. It's full of the most delicious recipes in the world, and it's one of the few cookbooks I've ever seen which actually tell you how to make everything from the beginning, step by step. Follow Mrs. Child's directions, and after you've hidden away your first few efforts at the bottom of the garbage can, presto!—you're suddenly an expert, for life.

32

The secret of successful entertaining, even for "impromptu" parties, is, in other words, *preparation*. Organization and preparation. Make some notes on the most important Dos and Don'ts for hostesses and guests. Before we're through we'll have a baker's dozen of them, but number one, naturally, for hostesses, is—plan ahead.

1. PLAN AHEAD. Make lists, lists, and more lists. Keep a pad and pencil in your purse wherever you go. Have a notebook for party ideas on your bedside table, so you won't forget all those brilliant notions that occur to you in the middle of the night. Make lists of people—people you enjoy, people you think would enjoy each other, people you are indebted to, people you'd like to know better. Then make shopping lists, lists of interesting menus, and preparation lists of things to do. If you're a working girl, play it smart and plan parties you can prepare for gradually during the last few days before D-day. Then make a list of last-minute details, so you won't get rattled just before the guests arrive.

2. SAVE TIME FOR YOURSELF. This means giving yourself *plenty* of time, so that you feel fresh, pretty, and self-confident when the party starts. When you look your best you're twice as glad to see other people. They sense your confidence, and instantly decide that this is going to be a good party—which, in turn, helps make it so.

Take a good look in the rear-view mirror, by the way, before you sally forth to meet your guests. A few months ago I was met at the door by a hostess who looked absolutely gorgeous in her long lamé dinner gown—but when she turned around she was even more spectacular. The hem of her skirt was caught up in her waistband, and she

33

was one of those women who never bothered to wear panties! This was before "bottomless" shows became the thing in San Francisco, so I quietly unhooked her skirt for her and said no more about it. But I always keep the incident in mind when my own doorbell rings.

Pre-party jitters? Some women take tranquilizers, others have a stout drink at the crucial moment—say, half an hour before the guests arrive, when the cat is discovered finishing off the pâté-and-caviar.

I don't recommend either pills or liquor. You never know what your reaction will be, in a time of stress. Try deep breathing instead. It's amazingly relaxing and, unlike artificial stimulants and depressants, it doesn't leave you gaga. Physical exertion is good, too, for party nerves. Stand on your head if you know how, and be sure to do it before the guests arrive or they'll think you didn't take my advice about the booze.

3. CONSIDER EVERY DETAIL OF YOUR SETTING. Think of it as if you were the director of a theatrical production. Do everything necessary to provide the atmosphere you want, and don't forget the important props that help the action along. Are the lights low and glamorous? (Try pink frosted bulbs in your lamps, which have a wonderfully softening effect on wrinkles and on tempers as well.) Be sure the candles are lighted and there are plenty of ashtrays. Repeat: *plenty* of ashtrays? Cigarettes? Matches?

Next, check your bar setup. Even with professional help it's amazing what can be overlooked. Olives and onions for the martinis? Slices of lemon peel? Lots of cocktail napkins? Ice? (Always have on hand at least twice as much ice as you think you will really need. A good hostess may be forgiven for running out of liquor occasionally, but ice—never!) Start your background music next. If it's live, the musicians should be tuning up. If you're playing records, select unobtrusive instrumental numbers, or if you've planned to play the FM radio, turn to a station that specializes in this sort of thing. Taped music is ideal. Many recorders will play for hours without being touched. You don't want to be *fussing* with your arrangements during the party.

Check the bathroom once more now, for clean guest towels, nice soap, a handsome water glass, and plenty of tissue. Make sure you didn't leave your razor on the edge of the tub as I did recently—or your bra hanging on the back of the bathroom door!

Close the kitchen door now, because you don't want backstage noises to intrude, spray a whiff of your favorite fragrance around the living-room and you are ready to welcome your guests.

4. ATTEND TO GREETINGS AND INTRODUCTIONS. This is the moment most apt to be dreaded, even by the experienced Party Girl. You must greet each arrival by name, and you must introduce early arrivals to one another. Unless you were born with the memory skills of a politician, this can be pretty tricky, and it's a bit of a juggling act to get the party going while you are busy welcoming new arrivals.

If you have trouble remembering names, ask a friend to help you practise beforehand. She gives you the first name and you have to supply the last. Then vice versa. Have her quiz you about the appearance of each guest—height, hair coloring, and so forth. Close your eyes as you say each name, and imagine the face that goes with it. This is a good time for making mental notes (or notes on paper, if you prefer) of special interests of your guests, topics of conversation to be encouraged or avoided, combinations of people who'd enjoy each other, and so forth.

Maybe, after all this homework, you'll still pull a blank. If so, don't agonize, just be frank and admit it. Laugh at yourself and say something light, such as "This is one of my best friends, whose name I can't remember at the moment." You'll be forgiven—eventually!

And do remember, it's the spirit of your welcome that really counts. You don't have to make like a cheerleader with pompoms and megaphone, but let your guests know that you are genuinely glad to see them. Offer a firm hand, a warm smile, and a sense of special greeting to each arrival. One delightful old baroness I know always says to her visitors, "Well, my goodness, am I ever glad to see *you!*" This is what's known as a royal welcome—and I must say it's marvelously effective. Keep it in mind when you welcome your guests.

If you have a guest of honor, be sure to stand near the entry with him (or her), introducing each new arrival, at the beginning of the party. After a reasonable time you and your honored guest may circulate, but you are responsible throughout the evening for the comfort and pleasure of the guest who is your party's *raison d'être*.

At a large party the hostess should not continue to introduce all guests to one another after the first ten or a dozen have arrived. It interrupts and annoys everyone involved. Far better to station yourself somewhere near the door, introducing new arrivals to just a few people, after showing them where to put their wraps. Always have a place planned where the coats can go—a handy closet, if possible, or an empty bed.

36

5. SEE TO THE CARE AND FEEDING OF YOUR GUESTS. Don't rush around in a flap, just quietly see to it that each guest is offered food and drink soon after being greeted. Prearrange a system for this, because a smooth performance is essential. You will need help of some sort if you're inviting a great many people, and each helper should know exactly what his duties are. You don't want your guests to be aware of the mechanical details; you want them to concentrate on having a good time. Everything should be effortless for them unless, of course, there is some amusing performance involved, such as an arrangement for guests to toast their own hors d'oeuvres over a little hibachi in the living room, or in your garden. Chips 'n dips are out, and so is anything else involving mess, clutter, and fuss, for yourself or for your guests, during the party.

Be sure to have plenty of nonalcoholic drinks on hand. Ginger ale, 7-Up, and tonic water are fine. San Francisco is known as a hard-drinking city, but in my own survey of a recent cocktail party here for twenty-four, six people (25 per cent) were nondrinkers. Remember, nondrinkers get thirsty too, and they appreciate having something to carry around and spill on the rug like everybody else!

If it's a dinner party, plan your seating well ahead of time. Make yourself a chart, or use place cards, so you don't have to babble at the crucial moment, "Now let's see, you sit next to Richard, and you—uh—no, wait a minute, that won't work either," while everybody stands around getting fidgety. If by chance you've forgotten to do this, it's better to leave your guests for a moment while you draw up a quick battle plan in the other room. The seating plan can make or break a large dinner party. I prefer place cards myself, even at rather small and informal parties. They look so nice, and they save a great deal of effort.

Try dividing your dinner party into two or more tables, and then give the men different seating assignments, one for the early courses, another for dessert and coffee. It's a great conversation-pepper-upper, and it gives the ladies a pleasant sensation of being pursued by a number of beaux. Watch the eyes begin to sparkle when the men change places, and listen to the decibel level rise! This is the Party Girl's answer to wife-swapping-in-lower-suburbia. And it's legal, too.

6. WATCH FOR DANGER SIGNS AMONG YOUR GUESTS. If good old Freddie is beginning to get that glazed look, whisper to the bartender to go slow on his drinks, and water them down a bit. Husband and wife beginning to make like snapping turtles? Separate them tactfully before they bite. Are your favorite Republican and Mister Big Democrat working themselves up to a full-scale brawl? Take one of them gently by the arm and say, with a wink, "Darling, there's someone over here I want you to meet, and you must tell her all about your rose garden. She *adores* flowers." He'll know exactly what you're doing, of course, but he'll be grateful to you. No one wants to go home from a party with a bleeding ulcer, or a black eye.

And speaking of flowers, watch out for the wallflower, male or female, at your parties. A young man can be just as shy as a girl about getting acquainted, and you don't want anyone to feel lost while you're playing hostess. Give the timid soul a special introduction to someone who needs a good audience, and they'll both be happy in no time at all.

Danger: A gaggle of women huddling together while the men compare golf scores across the room. Your party is well on its way to disaster, so—break it up. Women behave this way mainly in self-defense, therefore you should concentrate on distracting the men. Drag over the most dazzling glamour girl you have on hand, work your way into the male group, and begin asking interesting questions, such as "What do you do for recreation, boys?"

First thing you know, the topic has changed to something of general interest, and you can throw in the story about the defrocked priest who kept a five-woman seraglio and ran for public office on the platform "God Is Love." Or something of that sort. Just keep things lively, whatever you do. The women can always talk to each other on the telephone some other time, and the men can lunch together downtown.

So there are six "Dos" to help you function gracefully as a hostess. In brief order, consider six equally important "Don'ts":

1. DON'T OVERSELL YOUR SPACE. Give your guests a chance to move around, to see one another, and be seen. Glamour Girl didn't buy new pink satin pumps for this party just to have them stepped on in the crush. Hide your breakaway antiques for the evening, and shelve all the nonessential knickknacks. Tonight you're collecting people, not things. People need space, and a comfortable place to sit down when their feet get tired. Arrange a few chairs conveniently in corners at a large cocktail party, and beware of the Great Sofa Trap. If your primary seating arrangement consists of a heavy sofa with a heavy coffee table right in front of it, people will either avoid it

altogether or get themselves so thoroughly stuck that you won't be able to pry them loose the next morning. Provide table space in various spots, if possible, but by all means let's not have any of those "TV tables" at a large gathering. They're a menace to navigation, and they make the place look cluttery.

2. DON'T URGE YOUR GUESTS TO OVEREAT OR OVERDRINK. It isn't hospitable, and they won't thank you for it when they have indigestion later and a head full of bass drums and bumblebees the next morning. If it's a dinner party, serve light hors d'oeuvres with cocktails, and lure your guests to the dinner table long before they have reached the point of no return. I try to limit drinks to two rounds. At a cocktail party, provide plenty of nourishing food, and have hot coffee available. I think it's particularly nice to offer your guests a cup of hot bouillon or consommé before you turn them out into the night—providing, of course, that you hope to see them again. An evening of heavy drinking without proper nourishment can lead to disaster and you, as hostess, have a grave responsibility in the matter.

3. DON'T DRINK TOO MUCH YOURSELF—need I add? I have yet to see the hostess who can give a successful party while she's dancing around in the corner with a lampshade on her head. If you really feel the urge, wait till somebody else gives the kind of party where a little number like that will be appreciated.

4. DON'T MONOPOLIZE THE ATTENTION OF YOUR GUESTS, and don't cosset one or two favorites while the others go neglected. Tear yourself away from

that fascinating young man you've always wanted to spend three hours talking with. Drift around from group to group, making sure in a deft and inconspicuous way that everyone is happy and comfortable.

5. DON'T (on the other hand) BE A "HOSTESSY" HOSTESS. Don't fuss and fidget around, making your guests aware that this is all a terrible effort for you. Martyrdom as a spectator sport went out several centuries ago. You would rather be praised for skill than for effort, anyway. Skill always appears effortless; the truly feminine hostess manages, one way or another, to give the impression that this is all mere fun and games for her.

Your primary task as a hostess is to create an illusion, and guests should never be conscious of the method in your magic any more than theatre audiences should be disturbed by the creaking of backstage machinery. If you are your own cook and bottle-washer, do the cooking well ahead of time. The biggest "Hottray" you can afford is a splendid investment if you entertain without help. Never —but never—rinse dishes, scrape plates, or do any grubby chores of this sort during a party. Nothing is more dismaying to your guests, or more destructive of your personal glamour. Whisk the dirty plates and leftovers out of the way fast, close the kitchen door, and pretend to yourself that you have five maids and a butler out there. If a guest offers to help during the party, say, "Oh, I never wash those things, I just throw them away," smile firmly, and refuse to budge.

6. (AND MOST IMPORTANT OF ALL) DON'T APOLOGIZE! No matter what happens, don't succumb to this temptation; it only makes everyone uncomfortable.

41

So the living-room rug didn't come back from the cleaner's in time for the party? Who cares? Don't mention it. Tell yourself you *prefer* living with bare floors, and murmur vaguely, if anyone remarks on it, "I thought we might like to dance, later on . . ." So you forgot to turn on the casserole this afternoon, and there's nothing in the house to eat, when the guests arrive. Don't panic. Just call up the nearest we-deliver restaurant, and order chop suey. Or send your Party Buddy out for dozens of hamburgers, or chicken sandwiches, and call it a picnic. (More on Party Buddies later—they're invaluable friends to have around at moments like this.)

My friend Marjorie is known around town as "The Rain Queen" because she handled a really disastrous party situation with such admirable aplomb. It was a formal dinner party, and her guests, dazzling in their best silks and jewels, were just sitting down to prosciutto with melon when the ceiling directly above the dining-room table began to leak. Marjorie shrugged and moved her centerpiece (a bowl of lovely pink roses) to the crucial spot. The party continued—but so did the dripping, and now the wet stain on the ceiling began to spread formidably. Marjorie's reaction to this was to telephone the apartment manager and bring out some umbrellas for her guests as she served the zabaglione. Someone in the flat above had left his bath water running, and we were practically afloat by the time we retreated to the living room with our coffee. But we all thought it was hilarious, because Marjorie herself didn't get into a flap. She didn't dream of apologizing —it wasn't her fault, after all! Even if it had been, apologies would have served just to spoil the evening.

If you are complimented on your party, or on the dress you are wearing, by all means reply graciously. Don't say,

"Well, I do the best I can in this tiny place of mine" or "That old thing? Heavens, I've had it for years!" If you do you are belittling the judgment of the person who was kind enough to offer you a compliment. You put him in a position where he must insist, and go on at length about something which ought to be passed off lightly. It's much better to say, "I'm so glad you like it" or "How good of you to tell me." Then everyone is happy.

Those are my own twelve rules on how to be a successful Party Girl—six Dos and six Don'ts. Count them off on your fingers every time you give a party. And don't stop at twelve, either, because there's a lucky-thirteenth rule I haven't mentioned yet.

It's the most important rule of all, and I think it's implied in every other rule I've mentioned. *It's the extra bit of giving, the extra bit of loving care*, that counts in life, and in party-giving too. That's why I called this chapter "Baker's Dozen." If the baker likes you he always slips an extra cooky into the package, and if you like people in general you'll offer them more, not less, than they've bargained for. Back in Waurika the church used to give "pounding parties" designed to help feed the poverty-stricken minister's family. Always these good people brought my father a little more than the traditional pound of butter, pound of flour, and so forth, because it was a way of showing their devotion to him, and their appreciation for his good works.

Don't only do what's traditional, or only what's expected of you. You will certainly never be an outstanding hostess that way. Rules are helpful, but you alone can turn the trick of perfection. Create an atmosphere around you which is yours alone—in the arrangements you've made,

43

the people you've chosen, the care with which you've studied each detail of your party—and the sense of warmth and gaiety you communicate to your guests. Put your heart into it, and your party will be something no one else could have given.

Let's assume that you know the basic rules for being a good guest already. *Don't blow bubbles in the soup,* and *don't sing bawdy songs at the old ladies' tea party* (unless they're like some of the old ladies I know, in which case they might love it.) Always say *Thank you very much. I had a very nice time.* Most of us are taught these little refinements at an early age, and yet there are a good many important matters in connection with being a good guest that are all too often forgotten or ignored. Part of your career as a top-notch hostess will depend upon your skills as a guest, so I want to mention a few of these points:

1. REPLY PROMPTLY TO INVITATIONS. It is your first duty as a thoughtful guest to make a prompt reply to any invitation, and yet it is amazing how many people neglect to do this. As a hostess, you know how important it is, so don't be delinquent when it's your turn to play guest. Don't wait because you're not sure whether or not you'll make it to the party; telephone or write to the hostess immediately, explain the situation, and offer your regrets. If it is a seated dinner party, or a theatre party, for example, she may accept them and invite you another time instead. If the party is less formal, she may suggest that you "drop by at the last moment, if possible"—but this is her prerogative to decide, not yours. She must make her arrangements for the party in good time, and is deeply appreciative when a guest lets her know definitely, one way or another, as soon as possible.

2. PROPER INTRODUCTIONS are necessary for anyone you bring to the party. Of course you do not *ask* to bring anyone at all, unless the circumstances are very unusual. (For example, a single girl who has just become engaged may ask if it would be convenient for her to bring her fiancé; the hostess may not have been aware of the situation.) If you are told to bring a beau with you, let the hostess have his name well ahead of time, and see that he is introduced to her as soon as you arrive. It would be a bit awkward to discover that your dream man had been popped into a departing taxi by the butler because everyone was under the impression he'd crashed the party!

3. DRESS FOR THE OCCASION. Consult your hostess if there is any doubt in your mind about what would be appropriate. If it's a costume party, it's unpardonable not to wear one. They are fun if you have any sense of humor. Enter into the spirit of the thing, and enjoy yourself.

As for noncostume parties, by all means *dress up.* Your hostess hasn't knocked herself out preparing for this evening just to have you arrive looking as if you didn't give a damn. Any girl who goes to a dinner party in an old tweed suit ought to be spanked for it, I think. It's just plain thoughtless and insulting. Wear something pretty, *please!*

If you don't have time to change after work—then you're working too hard for somebody else, and not nearly hard enough for yourself. You owe it to your hostess, as well as yourself, to look fresh and lovely in the evening. Change in the ladies' room at the office, if convenient—change in the nearest telephone booth, if you must—but change, after work, into something soft and feminine. Your entire mood will lift instantly.

These so-called convertible costumes for working girls are grim, in my opinion. A girl can't convert her state of mind by taking off her jacket and adding a string of pearls—particularly if the skirt she's been wearing all day has a great bunch of wrinkles across the crotch. The look I like for evening is definitely the unwrinkled-crotch look. It's the smooth and flowing look, the soft look—soft fabrics, soft hairdo, the soft-touchable-you look. Keep a make-up kit at the office, so you can redo your face for the evening. Give yourself a quick damp-wash from head to foot with one of those moist, scented towelettes you can buy in sealed packages. Splash yourself lavishly with your favorite perfume, and slip into your evening dress. Whether it's an Estevez original or a simple little shift you whipped up yourself with bargain-basement cotton chiffon, you'll arrive at the party looking and feeling like a million dollars. And that's the way you ought to feel.

4. DO THANK YOUR HOSTESS WITH A GIFT, if this is your first invitation to her house, or if you are the guest of honor. Flowers are fine, but don't arrive with a great bunch of them clutched in your hands. Your poor hostess will have to drop everything and rush off to find a vase, or half a dozen vases, to arrange them in, just at the busiest moment of her evening.

If you are the guest of honor, and want to offer a substantial thank-you in flowers, telephone your hostess ahead of time. Ask her what colors would be suitable, and have your flowers delivered the morning of the party.

5. LOOK AROUND WHEN YOU ARRIVE. Not just to see who's there, but to study your surroundings: what is charming or original about the room you are in? What special arrangements has your hostess made for the party?

46

Notice the flowers, the food, the drinks, and above all, notice the dress your hostess is wearing! Then you can offer compliments to her which are sincere, as well as specific. For all you know, a kind word to her during the party might be a real boon. Under that smiling exterior she may be wondering why she ever dreamed up this party in the first place—wishing instead she were on a slow boat to Madagascar. Far too many people go through parties half-blind, whether or not they've been hitting the martinis; and this, I suppose, is a fault which guests and hostesses must share. So many parties are mediocre that people expect mediocrity—the damp cocktail glass with no napkin in sight, the music too loud, the faces dreary and glum under glaring overhead lights, the conversation hopelessly boring, the bartender out of ice. Learn from other people's mistakes, as well as your own, of course; but don't neglect to notice what is first-rate while you're at it.

6. THANK YOUR HOSTESS PERSONALLY. Do this, of course, before you leave, but you should also telephone the next day, or during the following week, to thank her again. Better yet, write her a nicely worded little note. I prefer writing and receiving notes. It's a formal practice which suggests extra care and effort, and at the same time it's actually a timesaver for busy people.

If you've done all this, and haven't set fire to the upholstery either, you'll probably be invited back sometime. And if that's what you have in mind, please remember some of these equally important "Don'ts":

1. DON'T ARRIVE "FASHIONABLY LATE" for a party. It isn't nice, and it isn't fashionable, either. It implies that you had more important things to do than to come

when you were invited. Don't dash in for "just one quick drink" at a cocktail party and then run along with "Ta-ta, we're off to the So-and-sos'." It's better manners not to come at all, unless you can stay for a decent interval and make yourself agreeable. If you just wanted "one quick drink" you should have bought yourself a shot of bourbon at the corner saloon. And if you have to leave early, you should have explained the circumstances to your hostess when you accepted her invitation. When you leave a party early, go quietly so as not to distract the other guests, and make your farewells to your hostess as unobtrusive as possible.

2. DON'T BURDEN YOUR HOSTESS. She'll be on the lookout for wallflowers, of course, but you needn't be one. Go to the party with a positive, enthusiastic attitude. Be glad to meet people, and offer them interesting tidbits of conversation which you may have dreamed up ahead of time—it's not against the rules. Communication is what parties are all about, so communicate. If small talk isn't your forte, try walking up to someone and just smiling instead. A smile is a form of communication which looks great on most people.

If you see a man who intrigues you, try this ploy—a perennial favorite with accomplished Party Girls: walk up to him, smile, and say "Hello." Indicate the fact that you need a light for your cigarette. When he comes at you with the Zippo, steady his hand with your hand, look him straight in the eye, and then say, in a low and pleasant sort of voice, "Thanks."

Two little words—but that hand-steadying bit is called Body Contact, and is said to have something to do with male-female relations. The low-and-pleasant voice is very important too. Make him lean forward a little to hear what

48

you're saying. Let him talk, listen carefully to what he says, and ask a few questions. If he has a wife, she will now appear and see to it that you are introduced to several attractive men on the other side of the room. If he doesn't have a wife, you have a lovely evening ahead of you. So any way you look at it, you can't lose.

3. DON'T MONOPOLIZE YOUR HOSTESS, or the guest of honor. They have other people to consider as well as you. And don't, if it's a small party, grab the floor and use the guests as a private audience all evening. Even if you're a genius, half an evening of this is more than enough. If you *are* a genius, by all means hire a hall and sell tickets.

4. DON'T BE UNCOOPERATIVE. That is, don't move against the general feeling of the party in any way that will be annoying to your hostess or other guests. Your hostess has tried to set a general tone for the evening. It's up to you to realize what this tone is, and cooperate. At some parties it is perfectly appropriate to kick off your shoes and sing "Brandy, Let Me Alone" at the top of your voice. At others this would be considered rather a nuisance. If the hostess is content to have people sitting around in front of the fire talking politics and books, don't wildly insist on a scavenger hunt or a game of charades. If she wants her guests to play charades, then get in there and play charades for all you're worth, no matter how much you hate it. Be a good sport at parties, and eventually you'll find someone who'll want to play your favorite game with you.

5. DON'T BRING YOUR PROBLEMS TO THE PARTY. I've actually had some guests arrive with long,

sad faces and say, "It's been such a ghastly day, Pat, I don't feel a bit in the party spirit." I'm tempted to say to them, "Well, why don't you run on home, and come back some other time when you're feeling more cheerful?" Your hostess is counting on you to help make things gay and interesting and pleasant. One gloomy guest can douse the spirit of an entire dinner party, so if you want to sing the blues, better stay home and curl up with a good violin.

6. DON'T, DON'T, DON'T BE "HELPFUL" TO YOUR HOSTESS. After all I've said about cooperating, I know this sounds odd. What I mean is, don't be Helpful Harriet. Helpful Harriet insists on running out to the kitchen, banging things all around, just when you had yourself and the other guests half convinced that Jeeves was in charge of everything. Helpful Harriet just loves to do dishes; she even borrows your apron if you have one, —or asks you in a loud tone of voice where it is if you haven't. You can't get Helpful Harriet out of the kitchen, even if you swear by all the martyred saints that a maid is coming in the morning to do everything. So there you are, stuck on K.P. with Harriet, while all your other guests fend for themselves in the living room.

Helpful Harriet leaps to her feet in the midst of the most delightful dinner-party conversation, and shrieks, "Do let me help you clear these dishes, please; you have so much to do," and that's where H.H. gives herself away. Obviously, if she really wanted to be helpful she would have asked you quietly ahead of time, "Would you like me to be in charge of clearing the table, or bringing in the coffee, perhaps?" And she would have taken a simple no for an answer. What Helpful Harriet *wants*, obviously, is attention and appreciation. Not having any clear sense of

50

herself as a woman, or any well-developed feminine charms, she seeks approval by performing domestic chores as conspicuously as possible.

That makes twelve rules for guests, but of course there's a Baker's Dozen involved here too. The good guest follows these simple rules of courtesy; the superb guest, who is in demand everywhere, brings a magic "extra" to the party, one that is difficult to define. You know people like this, no doubt—they walk into a room and suddenly everything comes alive. They radiate warmth and joy wherever they go. They are witty and kind, unfailingly interested in all sorts of people. They know how to talk, and they know how to listen. If you have a good number of people like this on your guest list, then you, as a hostess, are very lucky indeed.

Some superb guests are just born that way, I think—but without a doubt others are made, by their own efforts, by experience, imagination, and the will to please. If you are a modest soul, and can't think what sort of magic you might have to offer at a party, consider this: your hostess chose you, after all, and she wants you to be there. She is going to some trouble to please *you*. Surely you can reward her efforts, not only with heartfelt appreciation, but with that extra effort which means giving something of yourself to her party. Perhaps she thinks you will be interesting to certain of her other guests—try to find out which ones, then, and talk with them. Maybe she admires your ability to be a good listener. Take your steps toward confidence one at a time and begin with the fact of your hostess' confidence in you. That's a firm base on which the world's best parties have been built.

CHAPTER FOUR

Just What Kind of Party Were *You* Thinking of—Sir?

Theoretically speaking, an accomplished hostess can give a fine party any time, day or night. I've given late-late suppers that lasted until 4 A.M. and once long ago, in 1958 I think it was, in a spectacular fit of virtue I got up at five and gave a duck hunters' breakfast. Within reason, you can entertain successfully round the clock.

BREAKFAST. It's a good way to entertain a committee, for example, and get some work done while you enjoy yourself. It's a very practical time to entertain people who are in town for conventions and business meetings, too busy later in the day for social indulgence. Indulge your guests at breakfast. If you give them tender, loving care at the beginning of the day they will thank you for it hours later. There's nothing so memorable as an unexpected treat, so concentrate on offering the unusual to your breakfast guests. Present them with the charming little luxuries which are not part of one's ordinary, day-to-day existence. Go to a specialty market and find fresh fruits that are out of season—serve them in unusual combinations, or beautifully arranged in little glass bowls, on a nest of crushed ice with fresh mint leaves. Serve tall glasses of fresh-squeezed, *real* orange juice. If you serve scrambled eggs, fold in an extra tablespoon or two of butter and some fine-chopped herbs before bringing them to the table. Or try crêpes rolled up with some especially delicious jam or jelly, and sprinkled with powdered sugar. Eggs Benedict is a fabulous breakfast dish, but don't try it unless you're an experienced cook; it takes split-second timing and a certain amount of legwork. You don't want to be dashing in and out of the kitchen during your breakfast party. The mood should be relaxed and sumptuous. Lots of good, strong well-brewed coffee, of course (and you should have some coffee substitute on hand as well). Things to avoid: fake "Danish pastries" and boring coffee cakes, anything obviously canned or limp-frozen, fried eggs, doughnuts, and all the ordinary breakfast foods everyone is tired of.

Set the table with your prettiest linens in soft colors. Use your pottery plates and mugs and decorate the table with geraniums and daisies, or bring on the silver coffee set if you have one. Use your best white china plates, glass bowls, and make an arrangement of roses or carnations. One of the most charming breakfasts I've ever been to was given by a clever hostess who decorated her table with individual jam pots and sugar bowls filled with bright blue bachelor's buttons. Her china was the familiar Blue Willow pattern, set on a plain white linen cloth with huge white linen napkins she had made (and beautifully hemstitched) herself. The centerpiece was a splendid bowl of hothouse strawberries, big as plums, with leaves and stems attached. After feasting ourselves royally on trout with lemon-butter sauce and little Swedish pancakes,

54

we devoured the centerpiece; and each guest, upon departing, was given a bachelor's button boutonniere to wear the rest of the day—always a pleasant way of remembering a party.

COFFEE is a sociable habit and a coffee hour at home is a pleasant way to entertain other women. If you want to meet your neighbors or thank them for little kindnesses —or if you want to help welcome new arrivals in the community—consider the Coffee as a possibility. I had a great time one Halloween with a Witches' Coffee Party three friends and I gave together. We arranged to use the social room at our church, and sent out the following invitation anonymously:

> Come join us in the tradition
> Of Trick or Treat and superstition.
> It's a COFFEE we're having,
> And there are no hitches,
> It's being given, you know, by
> FOUR OLD WITCHES.

Corny as all get out—but why should the kids have all the fun on Halloween? We gave the time and place, but no names, and there was a good deal of speculation around town as to who the hostesses were. When our guests arrived they found the four of us in witches' hats, and the room decorated in the spirit of the holiday: chysanthemums in gold and orange, autumn leaves, pumpkins, and so forth. We drank coffee and tea, ate party sandwiches and assorted sweets and thoroughly enjoyed ourselves. Sometime I'd like to give a Halloween party in an honestto-goodness haunted house, or even better, a haunted castle.

BRUNCH is one of the best inventions ever made, and I often think it must have been dreamed up by a working girl. It figures. She cleans her apartment on Saturday, washes her hair, fixes fresh flowers, does her shopping, mends and presses her favorite party dress—and then, Sunday morning, not too late, not too early, she's in the mood to give a party. Sunday Brunch is the answer, too, for the girl who has plenty of imagination and practically nothing in the piggy bank. You don't have to serve a lot of liquor. You don't have to prepare a huge amount of elaborate food. You don't have to wear yourself out with involved arrangements—and yet it's an ideal way for a single girl to entertain a mixed group.

If you are timid about trying your first Brunch, pick a Sunday when some important away-from-home sports event is going to be on television, and invite your friends to come and watch it with you, on your own or a borrowed set. Don't ask people who brag about loathing baseball or football, of course—but this needn't be the entire point of the party. Little conversation groups will form here and there, some guests will immerse themselves in the Sunday paper, others will browse your bookshelves or walk your dog around the block with you. Be casual, let people relax, and don't try to organize things. People should be able to act out their lazy-Sunday feelings together, and enjoy one another's company in a quiet way.

The most popular drinks for brunches are gin fizzes, Bloody Marys, screwdrivers, and champagne. If your bank account is really low, beer or a chilled rosé wine is perfectly acceptable. Try serving beer and tomato juice in equal parts. Sounds peculiar, but it's good. After a round or two of drinks, bring on a nice casserole, plenty of coffee, hot rolls, and a bowl of fresh fruit with cheese and crackers for dessert. No wine is necessary with the meal, but you may prefer to solve your entire liquor problem by serving a delicious wine punch, or a large, steaming bowl of mulled wine, for everyone to dip into at leisure.

The whole thing is so simple, really, that you can spend most of your time relaxing and enjoying your guests. If you've invited them for eleven o'clock or noon, the party will break up some time during the late afternoon, and you'll have plenty of time to clean up and still get to bed at a decent hour. It's ever so much better for the girl who works than a Sunday Night Supper, which is apt to send you on to a new week with a bad case of post-party exhaustion.

That's the easy way, but if you want to go all out for a Brunch you can have a party theme, and create a colorful environment for your guests to frolic in. A Mexican Brunch, for example, could be just as gay as the Fiesta I mentioned earlier. Make yourself a Mexican hostess gown —they're easy if you sew, and if not, quite cheap to buy. Serve margaritas or sangría, to drink, and for your main course, Chilaquiles (Mexican-style scrambled eggs). On the record player, you might have Herb Alpert and his Tijuana Brass.

Or maybe you're in the mood to play Scarlett O'Hara. I gave a Down South Brunch one year that was such a success I repeated the whole thing with different guests on the day of the Kentucky Derby. Magnolia leaves and blossoms, huge pink summer roses and honeysuckle made a bower of my living room. Mint juleps were served to the guests as they arrived. I wore a dress of white organdy with pink roses cascading down the side, and had my hair done in long ringlets. Four teen-age friends came to help me cook and serve, wearing colorful cotton dresses and matching turbans they'd made themselves. We had hominy grits, eggs à la New Orleans (a name I invented for eggs basted in hollandaise sauce), Southern fried ham, buttermilk biscuits, and peppermint sherbet with fresh mint leaves. Rave notices, both times—and each time it took me a week to get rid of my Southern accent.

LUNCH is more formal than brunch, generally speaking. Most people enjoy the traditional weekend luncheon, with a mixed group, cocktails served beforehand, and the meal at one-thirty or so, with a good part of the afternoon spent in conversation. But how many times have we all heard our friends say, "Oh Lord, I have to go to a ladies' luncheon!" Or, still worse—"I have to give one!"

I am all in favor of having plenty of men in my life, and yet there are times when a ladies' luncheon is really necessary. And I've learned that they can be fun, if the hostess makes an effort to provide really delicious food, an unusual setting, and a good combination of people to converse with.

One enterprising San Francisco hostess, who usually entertains at fabulous evening parties with her husband, decided that it would be a nice change of pace to give a ladies' luncheon. So she did—in the local pool parlor! All the ladies arrived, as requested, wearing their best hats and little white gloves, they took one look at each other and burst out laughing. The entire party was hilarious and, needless to say, no one who was there will ever forget it. It's a good philosophy in general, I think, to make that extra effort where other women are involved. The camaraderie shared among women at a happy social occasion is apt to be long-lasting, and deeply appreciated by every participant.

I know a bachelor girl who went into a complete panic

at the idea of giving a ladies' luncheon. She telephoned in despair, "Pat, what shall I do? Mother is here from Ohio, with an ancient aunt of mine, and I've got to invite a whole lot of ladies for lunch. It's going to be such a bore, and they'll be so critical of everything, I know!" Now this was absurd because Peg is a fine hostess, a superb cook, and a very intelligent girl. She was just having a conditioned-reflex kind of reaction, to what everybody *else* says, about ladies' luncheons. I told her to calm down, and apply the same principles at her luncheon which work so well at all the other parties she gives. We worked out the details together, and produced a party that was an outstanding success.

Since both honored guests were visitors in the city, we decided upon a "San Francisco" theme for Peg's luncheon. We constructed miniature versions of San Francisco's famous flower stands in her foyer and filled them with pots of marigolds and daisies. The luncheon table was done in the Chinatown manner with inexpensive decorations we picked up there (Peg put them away for future parties) and a centerpiece of pink azaleas in a handsome brass bowl. We made a tablecloth and matching napkins of polished orange cotton and tiny dragons held the place cards.

Crab Tetrazzini and our local sourdough "French bread" were on the menu, then a limestone lettuce salad, and back to Chinatown with a dessert of chilled loquats and lichee nuts, marinated ever so lightly in kirsch and served on a bed of crushed ice. The ladies gasped with pleasure over our menu, and thoroughly enjoyed the Chinese fortune cookies Peg provided with coffee. These are always fun, no matter what the age or composition of your group. The hostess who had dreaded her ladies' luncheon was soon basking in compliments, for each guest

59

was touched and delighted that a younger woman would go to so much trouble for the pleasure of the group. I love older ladies myself, and find them wonderful to work with. They often have a kind of wit and daring and a free-wheeling approach to life that put the younger set to shame.

Peg told me that one of her most formidable guests had gone straight home after the party and telephoned her son, an attractive bachelor, "I have just met a most charming and capable young lady. She entertains beautifully and is so thoughtful of her guests. I expect you to be here next Thursday evening at cocktails, to meet her." The only reason Peg didn't marry him was that she decided after several months that he still loved Mummy best. But they had lots of fun in the meantime.

PICNICS are a fine way for the single girl to get better acquainted with her gentlemen friends. For this reason every girl should be the owner of a really superb picnic basket. If your rich uncle dies and leaves you General Motors stock, by all means sell it and buy yourself a handsome $200-dollar fitted picnic hamper instead. If you're fresh out of rich uncles, go to the five-and-dime and buy yourself a 99-cent basket instead. Line it with a pretty print and fill it up with sumptuous surprises. Chilled wine, or champagne, with long-stemmed crystal glasses wrapped in linen napkins. Mushrooms stuffed with pâté, cold asparagus sprinkled with dill, herring in sour cream, Cornish game hen with a little carving board and knife to cut it—French bread, scallions, Port Salud. That's the fare which makes a picnic unforgettable.

Needless to say, you don't wear your jeans to this banquet. Put on your prettiest cotton dress and a big straw

60

hat, or flowers in your hair. I like gingham and ruffles for the country. Bring colorful cushions to lounge on and a tablecloth to spread on the grass. If you have a portable phonograph, so much the better; you'll be able to spend the afternoon listening to music while the clouds sail overhead.

Sometimes, even in sunny California, it isn't picnic weather, but don't let that stop you. Give a picnic right in your living room if you're in the mood. Spread out your tablecloth and cushions in front of the fireplace—it's cozy and fun on a rainy day.

Picnics for numbers of people can be given quite easily, indoors or outdoors, rain or shine, if you follow the simple expedient of making up individual baskets for your guests. One lady I know gives charming picnics for her grandchildren and their friends, with an absolute minimum of fuss and muss. She buys a number of inexpensive straw cowboy hats and cotton bandannas, wraps each child's portion in the bandanna, and serves it to him neatly stowed in the crown of the straw hat. After the feast the bandanna and hat are his to play with and take home. What could be simpler? "Grammie" is adored by children for miles around, and you can see why!

TEA . . . another "inevitable" on the Party Girl's social calendar, so make it elegant and beautiful. Of course you may decide to give a Mad Hatter's Tea Party, with everyone competing for honors in wild headgear. But more usually it's a formal occasion, and it often works best as a party for two generations or more. Invite friends your own age and older women too, as well as their daughters and your teen-age friends. Ask several of your best friends, in advance, to "pour." This is considered an

honor, and they will be delighted to help you. Be sure to
have two groups chosen to take turns at each end of the
table, because coffee is always served, as well as tea (or
perhaps a punch, in very hot weather).

At a tea party use your nicest linens. Serve tiny sandwiches, and let your guests feast their eyes, as well as their
appetites, on an array of cupcakes or petits-fours frosted
in rainbow colors. Have plenty of fresh flowers in big
bowls everywhere, and don't forget to wear something
smashingly pretty yourself. Teas are so nice to look at, it's
no wonder they are part of the repertoire of great hostesses everywhere.

AT-HOMES AND OPEN HOUSES are pleasant ways for
single people and couples to entertain. It's a good idea to
establish a regular pattern of them—perhaps once a year,
on a special occasion, so that you can keep in touch with
people you don't see very often otherwise. Thus your
party becomes a happy tradition to your guests and everyone looks forward to the date. Many a traditional party in
the older sections of the country has been going for fifty
or seventy-five years, with children and grandchildren of
the original hosts now presiding; I know of one Christmas
party in an Eastern city which became so large, after four
generations, that the family had to "hire a hall"—the ballroom of the local tennis club—and still it is everyone's
favorite party of the year.

Begin by asking a few neighbors and their friends to
stop by with their families, and keep the arrangements
quite simple. It's fine to serve a punch and this kind of
party is inexpensive, because there's no need to provide
other liquor; just be sure to have plenty of nonalcoholic
beverages on hand and plenty of glasses and ice. Offer an
attractive arrangement of finger food on a table or side-

board near the punch. At Christmas or New Year's, egg-nog would be ideal, with fruit cake and Christmas cookies.

You won't need any help with this party unless, of course, it turns out to be very large. Don't include too many hours in your "Open House" invitation; it can be quite tiring to stand on hostess duty for a long period of time. Three or four hours is enough. And if you are a guest on such an occasion, don't linger too long. You're expected to drop in for a little while, share a bit of conversation and good cheer, have something to eat and drink; and then—goodbye!

SHOWERS. If you're going to give a shower, stop and think a bit about what kind of party your guest of honor most *enjoys*. A shower can be given at any time, day or evening; and the idea is to please the one who's being honored, not only by gift-giving, but by seeing to it that everybody has a wonderful time.

I've been to some unforgettable showers. There was the one we gave in Sulphur, Oklahoma, for our teacher, Miss Cramer, who was about to get married. It was a great party with good company, plenty of singing, dancing, delicious food, and we made merry until the wee hours of the morning. My contribution to Miss Cramer's trousseau was a Clabber Girl premium cookbook—I had no money for anything better—and Miss Cramer told me that was exactly what she had wanted all her life. At a shower, it's the spirit that counts.

Recently I went to another shower that was along much the same lines. It was in Dean Martin's house in Hollywood, given by Mrs. Martin, Mrs. Milton Berle, and Janet Leigh, in honor of Jerry Gershwin and his wife. "The Monkees" provided music for our dancing this time, and all of us—including Marge and Gower Champion, Polly Bergen, Bob Wagner, and Eddie Fisher—had a whale of a good time.

Dean had to be away that evening taping a show, but he came in later, gave us a smile and a wave, and went upstairs to rest. People in show business work hard, and if they're successful at it, their schedules are apt to be really grueling. I wouldn't have disturbed Dean for anything in the world that evening, but as it happened, I did have a funny little conversation with him, quite by mistake. I went upstairs trying to find the powder room and managed to blunder into the master bedroom instead.

"Hi" said Dean and, although I tried to make myself scarce, he insisted that I stay and chat a bit. He remembered that I'd had to follow his act with a fashion show the summer I managed the shop at Cal-Neva—on the same stage where he and Frank Sinatra had performed the night before. "How did it go?" he asked me.

"Well, I couldn't follow you without a glass in my hand," I told him, "so I came out on stage with a glass of milk and proposed a toast to the American Dairy Association."

Dean didn't automatically try to top this—instead he laughed as if he had never heard anything funnier in his life. I thought again, then, of that adorable Miss Cramer, who made me feel that my pathetic little offering was as good as a heap of diamonds. The art of graciousness is a lovely thing indeed.

There are all sorts of ways for people to enjoy themselves at showers, and it's up to you to provide the possibilities. If you haven't got Dean Martin in the master bedroom, alas, you'll just have to use your imagination and think of something else that might be fun.

64

How about a wine-tasting party, for example? It's a pleasant way for the bride-elect and her fiancé to entertain. If you live in California you might even be able to persuade a wine company to supply you with everything you need: wine, tasting tables, and colorful posters for your decor. The procedure is to have various kinds of wine, white and red, sweet and dry, to taste, in glasses poured only about one-third full. Plates of bread and cheese are on the table too, so that your guests can prepare their palates afresh for each new tasting. Those who take it seriously refrain from smoking during the procedure, and you should see to it that wine-tasting does not take place in a smoke-filled room.

Guests could bring gifts of various sorts for the bridal couple to this kind of shower: wine racks, glasses, coasters, corkscrews, and all the accessories—as well as bottles of rare and delicious vintage wine. Decorate your table with linens dyed claret or burgundy-color, and have bowls of real grapes with fresh grape leaves if you can get them.

The gifts most dearly prized are those that come from the heart, so next time you give a shower see how clever you can be. For example, you might invite your guests to a gourmet luncheon and ask each one to bring for the bride her own favorite recipe—something she has invented herself, perhaps, or something which has been a family secret for years. Special ingredients for these gourmet dishes may be provided too, if the donor wishes, but the true gift, or course, is the sharing of feminine lore—the welcoming of the new bride into the company of women who know how to do things beautifully.

COCKTAIL PARTIES are much maligned, and often rightly so. But they are still the best way, in our society, to meet people. If you're a single girl, new in town, you'll find them well worth going to. They're well worth giving too, for many reasons—although we have to face the fact that it's an expensive way to entertain. How else are you going to gather such a large group of people together, such a mixture of all ages and all types, so casually and comfortably? How else can you repay social obligations so painlessly, how can you introduce your friends to each other in such large numbers, and how better can you show certain men who fascinate you that they ought to be fascinated in return? Then, too, in a busy life, one does get involved with a certain number of people who are rather blah, though there is nothing really wrong with them. If they are well mixed at a cocktail party, with others who have more to offer, then no one has to suffer. I wouldn't advise asking anyone you actively dislike to a party in your home for any reason; still, let's admit that the cocktail party is first and foremost a socially useful form of entertainment.

The rules in Chapter 3 will help you give a first-rate cocktail party, the kind people don't want to leave—the kind they talk about the next day, the next month and the next year. Whatever you do, don't give a *mediocre* party. They're so forgettable! If you have to give a bad party, by all means give a really frightful one and get it out of your system. Just for fun—and to check over some of the major points involved—here's how:

HOW TO GIVE A TERRIBLE COCKTAIL PARTY

1. Come home from work late and exhausted on Party Day. Nothing has been planned ahead of time, of course —you believe in the Spontaneous Combustion Theory of Partygiving. There's a pile of laundry in the front

hall, and lots of dead flowers standing around in all the vases, just to help get things started. You've forgotten to order the liquor (the first guests to arrive can go out and buy it for you) and you've made sure that all major plumbing fixtures are out of order.

2. Now, have three stiff drinks to brace yourself. Don't wash (there isn't time), just slip into something really hideous. The well-wrinkled wool skirt you've been wearing all day will do; add a dark blouse that will show off your white underwear properly at the neckline, and tie a dirty apron around your waist. Leave one hair clip or curler somewhere around the back of your head, for rear-view interest.

3. Make sure all the overhead lights are blazing, so your female guests will look as if they had just been exhumed from the grave, and the men will bristle nicely with five-o'clock shadow.

The Hidden Bar Ploy: stash the liquor away someplace down low in the kitchen, put the ice in a drippy washtub at the far end of the dining room, and enlist an eighty-five-year-old teetotaler relative as bartender.

Background music: loud, so no one can hear a word of conversation.

Ashtrays: you haven't any. In the bathroom, leave one slimy piece of soap the size of an almond, no towels, no tissue, no nothin'.

4. Don't introduce anyone (and avoid speaking to arriving guests yourself) until the party is well under way. Then interrupt everyone and call for total silence as you, waving your seventh martini for emphasis, introduce each guest all the way around the room. Scramble as many names as possible. (It shouldn't be difficult, at this point!)

Don't introduce anyone at all to the guest of honor. You haven't invited anyone he would want to meet, anyway.

67

5. Serve little plates and slippery bowls loaded with chips 'n drips. Make a big deal out of it. Dash back and forth from the kitchen frantically replenishing your supplies. Interrupt the conversation constantly to ask your guests whether they have had enough to eat and drink. When they say yes, argue with them. When they get cross, apologize. Tell them what a hard life you have. Make sure everybody is paying strict attention to *you* at all times.

6. You've invited a fascinating combination of people to your party, of course: three old ladies from the Christian Temperance Union, several couples who were recently indicted on wife-swapping charges, your local minister, several hippies in beards and sandals, the head of the local unit of the John Birch Society, your favorite author, the critic who panned his last book, and the lady from downstairs who speaks nothing but Russian.

Now, if the party is starting to swing in spite of your heroic efforts to prevent it, get in there and drag all the glamorous females off into a corner with you. Start an insistent conversation about (a) the difficulty of finding a really good dry-cleaner who will work for a reasonable price these days, (b) the last operation your sister's mother-in-law had, and why it wasn't a success, or (c) the long, long trip a friend of yours once took to Passaic, New Jersey, and how she didn't like it very much when she got there.

Congratulations! Your party is now dead, and you will never have to give another one. If you send out invitations, everyone will leave town.

What you need at this point is a friend, so let's turn hastily to the subject of "Party Buddies." At cocktail parties the beau who is not romantically involved with you can be your most treasured pal and partner. Ask him to play the role of host, helping your bartender if you have one, and if not, serving at the least the first round of drinks himself. Count on him to help you in situations where a single girl feels timid at times: in case of party crashers, for example, or overenthusiastic drinkers who threaten to get out of hand. Since this is a trusted friend you can explain to him that your plans are flexible for the evening. After the party maybe the two of you will go out to supper together, or share a casserole at home and talk over the party. But if you are invited out by someone new and promising after the party, then it is understood that you are free to go. You may help your Party Buddy in return, by doing hostess duties at his next party if he wishes.

What if you are going out with several different men at the moment? Should you invite them all to the same cocktail party? Well, lucky you, but my advice is to ask only one of them per party, and make that one your special date for the evening.

DINNER. Single girls generally find cocktail parties easy to give, but they are afraid of dinners. Young marrieds, too, feel that way. And yet you needn't be apprehensive; it's just a matter of thinking the thing through, and getting yourself organized. Start small, as I've suggested, and keep things very simple at first. Buy yourself a little notebook if you really want to do things right, and keep a chart of duties for dinner party preparation, from menu-planning and house-cleaning all the way down to lump sugar for the demi-tasses. Then, the morning after each party you give, when the details are still fresh in your mind, write a memo for yourself, listing what you did right and what you did wrong. Ask yourself how you could improve the situation, or your own performance, next time. Note the food you served, and your guest list, so that you won't serve beef Stroganoff every time the Baileys come for dinner, and so you'll remember that Elizabeth W. likes vodka, not gin, in her martinis. Make a note of your sad discovery that Mr. D. is allergic to crab. It's the hostess who *remembers*, who makes the grades. And, in your little notebook, remark, too, upon the people who seemed to enjoy one another's company particularly. Such a list of comments can be invaluable to you in planning future parties.

DANCES. Well, why not? They're not just for teenagers. People of all ages like to dance, and all you really need to give a ball of your own is plenty of floor space and good music. Clear all the furniture out of one or two rooms, and if you still have space for some chairs around the edges, or a small group of tables and chairs, the party is on. Taped, recorded or live, your music should be danceable, of course. If you have a band, be sure to audition carefully—good listening music is often far from ideal for dancing purposes. If you're using a hi-fi, be sure it is in proper working order. Nothing is worse than the ear-splitting shriek of a set that is on the blink.

There should be a room available where the guests can relax and converse away from the sound and action, and if your group likes games as well as dancing, have some tables set up there for bridge and dominoes. You may want to give a dinner dance, in which case it is better to plan background music only until the meal has been served. Jumping up and down to dance during a formal meal is hard on the digestion, and hard on the help too; besides, all that lovely food is sitting there half the time, getting cold.

A supper dance is easier to give, and often, I think, more

fun. Invite guests for nine o'clock or later. Have the music going when they arrive and plan to dance until midnight or so. At that time serve a buffet supper. The mood can be as formal as you like, or you can go native with Greek or Latin American rhythms, and have a party theme to match. Dancing fads come and go, and if there's something new and lively on the Party Scene just now, you might ask a local school of dance to send over an instructor for the evening. Your guests will enjoy learning the new steps, and you can often make this arrangement free of charge, because of the customers the school hopes to gain. Make sure, if you choose to have demonstration dancers at your party, that they don't just demonstrate, while the guests sit and watch. It's more fun when everybody gets into the act.

SUPPER. Few people realize it, but an intimate little supper after a dance, after the theatre, after practically anything, can be a hostess' secret weapon in the entertaining game. There's something very special about a supper, and I suppose it's partly because we all expect to stop by at a restaurant, or some other public place, for that late-late snack. It is such a pleasant surprise to find ourselves in a private home instead—no waiter fussing with the ashtrays to let you know that he wants you to go home—and firelight, candlelight, and a cozy feeling of being awake with a chosen little group of friends, while the rest of the city is sleeping.

Supper parties are simple and inexpensive to give. You won't need much in the way of liquor. Your preparation list should include fresh flowers, fresh linens, freshly brewed coffee, candles for every candle holder, and a light but delicious little meal to eat. Oyster stew, eggs Benedict,

71

or cheese fondue are nice for a group, and yet, for a supper party *à deux*, there's nothing nicer than plain old scrambled eggs, plain old English muffins, and plain old champagne.

One thing is really grim about the dating game, as it's played by far too many people. The girls want "status" on their dates, and expect to be taken to fancy restaurants and nightclubs every time they go out with a man. I've noticed that men are really apt to get confused if they are offered a taste of simple, old-fashioned hospitality instead. And that's too bad. After all, there are still plenty of girls left in the world who don't want to dig a man for expenses and prestige. They want to be gracious and friendly, and they are perfectly willing to take some of the burden of entertaining a man they happen to like.

I never know when I am going to meet a man I really like, so I try to keep my apartment ready at all times for unexpected visitors. There's always food for snacks, polished silver for the table, clean place mats in pretty colors, and fresh linen napkins. I keep a couple of bottles of champagne in the refrigerator, too—California brands such as Le Domaine are quite delicious, and well within the budget of the working girl.

One night I went out with a very attractive young electronics executive, friend of a friend of mine, who was visiting from New York. Dutifully he took me to several nightclubs, but we didn't pay much attention to the floor shows, we were so busy talking. Around midnight he suggested that we go somewhere for a bite to eat. I said, "Yes, let's go to my apartment, and I'll cook some scrambled eggs for you."

Well, you should have seen the look on his face, but he

didn't argue, so we came back to my apartment. He opened the champagne while I went into my eggs-and-muffins routine. Three hours later we were still talking. He was a marvelous man to talk to, and it dawned on him eventually that was what I really wanted to do. He realized that I wasn't teasing, and so he was quite comfortable about it.

When he left me at 3 A.M. he said, "Pat, maybe I shouldn't tell you this, but when you suggested coming to your apartment I assumed it was a come-on. It's been so long since a girl offered to cook for me that I couldn't believe it. Thanks so much, my dear; this will be one of my happiest memories of San Francisco." Then he kissed me goodnight, and added, "Next time I'm in town we're not going to begin the evening in those damned noisy places, we're going to begin it right here, you understand?" The following day I found four dozen long-stemmed red roses on my doorstep with his card.

The girl who knows how to be a gracious hostess, be it 3 p.m. or 3 a.m., with a crowd in a ballroom or alone with one man in her apartment, is the girl who can call the plays the way she wants them—and the passes too. She's poised because she's sure of her skills, and she has the confidence of self-respect.

The girl who has nothing to offer a man but a fast bounce in the hay is going noplace. And the girl who feels obligated is already there. If you can give a man comfort, beauty and warmth as a hostess in your own home, then he will consider your worth as a person, rather than seeing you just as a sex object. All normal girls want to be sexy, but there isn't a person on earth, male or female, who wants to be thought of as an object. Most of us would agree that the greatest party in the world is no substitute for a session in the boudoir with a man who really turns us on; but the fact remains—an accomplished Party Girl has given herself a valuable sort of free choice in the matter. With all of her feminine skills developed to their highest degree, she can save sex for when she really means it.

CHAPTER FIVE

Why is Everyone Naked, Mother?

"Why is everyone naked, Mother?"

"Hush, dear, Mother's giving a party."

"But why didn't anyone wear any clothes?"

"Shh, darling, this is a Garden of Eden Party. You'll understand when you're a little older. Run along, now."

"Waaah, I wanna come to the party too!"

That's the way it goes—if you give parties with really interesting themes everybody wants to get into the act. If your friends are exhibitionists with gorgeous figures, by all means give a Garden of Eden Party. Otherwise do some thinking, before you give a party, about another theme that might be appropriate. The list of possible themes is as large as your imagination. And the more memorable the theme the more memorable your party will be.

Everybody loves a theme which allows the guests to dress up (or down) and enter a temporary world of make-believe. Don't be afraid of corn—try a Kansas Harvest Moon Festival. Be far-out, and give a Space Safari. Be topical, historical, farcical, traditional or sentimental.

However you do it, the idea is to capture the imagination of your guests; then follow out your theme, in décor, refreshments and entertainment, to the last practical detail.

Suppose you read in the newspaper one morning that a rarely seen comet is approaching Earth, and will be visible on a certain evening a few weeks off. Do you yawn and go on to the stock-market reports and the obituaries? Not if you're a Party Girl. You telephone the City Fathers (every city has an assortment of Fathers tucked away in those big gray buildings downtown) and you ask them if they would like to lend you the Planetarium, for a Comet-Viewing Party. It never hurts to ask, and you never know when civic leaders or businessmen are looking for a way to publicize their activities—to advertise, in effect, without running an ad. This is the sort of thing they sometimes like to do through private parties, and if you are an accomplished hostess they will be delighted to have your interest and cooperation.

If the Planetarium isn't available, never mind. Go ahead with your celestial party at home. Arrange a darkened corner by the window, on a balcony, or in the garden, and borrow a telescope. Hang printed plastic foam balls from the ceiling of your living room, in graduated sizes, labeled with the planets' names. String up twinkling "star lights" in a network across your ceiling, and ask your guests to come costumed as space travelers, or as they think people on far planets might look. Play far-out "space music" on the hi-fi or tape recorder, and serve exotic drinks no one has ever tasted before.

Maybe you and your friends prefer astrology. After my Mexican Fiesta, when my career as a Party Girl had been launched with such a great splash, everyone was wondering what I would do next. And so was I, of course . . . I suppose all that guessing about the future explains why my next effort was an Astrology Party. I asked each guest to let me know the date of his or her birth well ahead of time, so there was no doubt about the theme of the party from the start. Practically no one told the year, of course, but I did learn enough to discover everyone's zodiac signs, and each guest was tagged upon arrival with the proper classification. I've never seen conversation explode so fast at a party. Geminis were finding soul mates in other Geminis they'd never seen before, and Scorpios were confessing to other Scorpios that no one else had ever really understood them.

I had emptied both bedrooms of furniture and installed tents of striped felt. A palmist held forth in one tent, an astrologer in the other. A tarot-card reader told fortunes in the living room, and on the dining table was a huge crystal ball, borrowed from an antique shop. Sitting beside this object was a man who gazed at it so fanatically that I was accused of hiring a television fiend and then not giving him a set to look at. Actually, the "talent" that evening donated their services for the sheer fun of it, and in the hope of picking up some regular clients—which I'm sure they did. Everything worked out beautifully, except that in all the excitement I forgot to offer the tarot reader a drink, and she left the party in an occult rage.

Everyone wondered, that evening, about the palmist who made such uncanny pronouncements about all my guests, and I guess this is as good a time as any to confess his secret. He was a doctor friend of mine, all bundled up in heavy robes and veilings, and he was able to "diagnose" a good many secrets by studying skin texture of the hand and other physical signs. Then too, it happened that many of the guests were patients of his. Talent lurks everywhere, you see. If you invite interesting people to your parties they may want to exchange professions, as well as telephone numbers, before the evening is over.

When you're looking for inspiration on this matter of party themes be sure to consider the latest fads, and make use of them while they're really new. It was a coup to give the first James Bond Party, but imitation in this field is boring. In San Francisco the first Bond party was given by an authentic private eye. He sent his invitations in code, on Western Union blanks: 1 stood for A, 2 for B, and so forth, so the message was not too hard to figure out. Unfortunately, his guests outdid him in this department, and sent their replies in such complicated codes that he really didn't know who was going to show up until they arrived!

If you're inspired by the latest detective hero on TV or in the movies, you can always send your invitations in the form of legal summonses. A friend of mine did this for a party at a North Beach nightclub that's rigged up as an imitation jail, complete with paddy wagons and sirens sounding. For some of the guests the whole thing was just a little too realistic, though. Several men took one look at the summons and left town, thinking their ex-wives' lawyers had finally caught up with them. You have to match your theme rather carefully to the guest list you have in mind. Be sure to let your guests know in the invitation exactly what's expected of them, too. It's always a bit awkward if someone shows up dressed in psychedelic body paint for a black-tie dinner.

The calendar presents all kinds of ideas to the imaginative Party Girl. I know one clever hostess who gives a Columbus Day party every October 12, and another who celebrates Chinese New Year's with her friends each year, by renting a couple of rooms in a Grant Avenue hotel in

San Francisco so that everyone can watch the Chinatown parade. Although this parade is one of San Francisco's outstanding events, many people never get to see it because it's so crowded below in the streets. My friend provides a comfortable grandstand for her guests, and they watch, drinks in hand, with egg rolls and barbecued spare ribs to nibble on, while the firecrackers and dragons and drum corps wend their way through the streets below. The owner of a charming New York apartment does the same sort of thing annually for his friends and their children on the day of the Macy's Christmas Parade. Everyone is comfortable and the view is perfect, as it happens, from his living-room windows. It's a nice way, I think, to entertain a family group on a traditional occasion.

I'm all for traditional parties, but you needn't wait until Christmas rolls around. Think of all the other possibilities! Who could resist an invitation to a party in honor of Martha Washington's birthday on April 6 instead of George's on February 22? And think of the color and costumes involved in a celebration on August 25 of the birthday of Margaret Mitchell, who wrote *Gone with the Wind!* My own birthday is December 26, so I prefer to give birthday parties for my friends. . . .

If you're celebrating a friend's birthday, by all means be as sentimental as you please. I've found that it's always fun to dig up old photographs and ask guests to come in costumes from the good old days. Plaster your photographs around the room, or pin them up on a screen for everyone to enjoy. You can order from one of those mail-order specialty shops copies of the headlines from the day your guest of honor was born. Rummage around in salvage shops for old magazines, posters, advertisements, and other mementos of the past. Anniversaries can be celebrated sentimentally this way too. You'll want to have as many of the wedding photographs as possible on hand, of course—and invite members of the original wedding party.

Most people love a party that is unashamedly sentimental. Nothing is more tiresome than the person who plays it cool all the time, so don't! Parties should be warm, not cool. Christmas should be celebrated with yule logs in the fireplace, the smell of evergreen, plenty of tinsel and glitter, and the sound of all the old familiar carols. Easter is for soap-shiny children in their springtime finery, rolling eggs on the lawn. The Fourth of July is for John Philip Souza records, flag-flying, sparklers, and bunting of red, white and blue.

Each Thanksgiving and Christmas I have dinner parties for all the people I know who are a long way from home. Don't let yourself be lonely during the holidays—not with so many others in the city cut adrift. Get together with your friends and have a good time.

One group I know did this several years ago at Thanksgiving, and now they have a full-fledged tradition going. Each year they divide the chores and the expenses of an elegant, old-fashioned Thanksgiving Party. They hire a bartender and a maid months ahead, since help is impossible to get on short notice over the holidays. The turkeys are cooked by a caterer, and other cooking jobs are divided among the various families involved. The women take care of flower arrangements, and the men order wines and liquors, and do the heavy work of setting up tables and moving furniture.

No one in the group has a home large enough for a gathering of twenty-four, so they meet for cocktails in one apartment, and then move nearby to another home, where the tables are waiting, beautifully decorated in the traditional Thanksgiving manner. The women wear long dresses, and the men are resplendent in their dinner jackets. After dinner they dance, and the maid does the dishes. She is well worth every cent of the holiday rate, of course, since the aftermath of a Thanksgiving Party can be pretty grim in the kitchen.

A party on this scale costs $200, more or less, depending on the prices and wages in your area. Split this twenty-four ways, though, and it's a good price to pay for cocktails and wines, a delicious dinner, good service, and a companionable Thanksgiving.

One of my most memorable parties was a Christmas black-tie dinner for forty, given on December 19. Invitations set the mood for the party: quietly formal, they were written in script and decorated with a simple, old-fashioned green wreath. Truman Capote's tender story "A Christmas Memory" was my inspiration, and like the people in the story I worked for weeks in advance to prepare for my party. My artistic friends helped me with cut-outs of angels, dolls and animals for our Christmas trees. I found a high-school choir group that was delighted to sing carols at the party. The cost of "live" music is often prohibitive, but never underestimate the desire of an enthusiastic singing group for an audience. This fine choir of young people donated its services, and rehearsed for weeks the songs we chose for the party.

The angelic young singers in their red robes were caroling outdoors on my front balcony as the guests arrived that crisp December night, and this set the mood of my party, exactly as I had hoped. The group included a good many lively members of the Jet Set, who were more quiet than usual that evening—not subdued, just happy to be with their friends at Christmas time.

My apartment was decorated, of course, in the traditional Christmas manner. I had three fresh, fragrant firs, one in the foyer, one in the living room, one in the dining room. There were swags of greenery too, here and there. For this party I borrowed the apartment upstairs, so we could have cocktails in my own apartment, then dine formally above. The choir stood singing on the stairs during the cocktail period, and then followed us upstairs to sing during the early part of dinner. A violinist arrived at this point, to add to the warmth and color of the Christmas music.

At dinner we were served by the bartender and two maids. We sat at round tables covered with cloths of a rich maroon paisley print, with napkins to match. The table linens were much admired, which pleased me, since I had made them myself! No one noticed that the cloths were not even hemmed; and the napkins looked finished enough, with their edges fringed. It's the effect that counts, so never waste time on nonessential details. I had a miniature Christmas tree as centerpiece at each table, a larger one on the buffet table, which was also covered with paisley print. Trader Vic's famous Chinese ovens cooked the roast suckling pig for me, but everything else was prepared at home—wild rice, artichoke hearts filled with spinach, heart-of-palm salad, and so forth. It was a true Christmas feast!

Two more musicians came in to join the violinist after dinner, and we danced and chatted and wished each other a Merry Christmas, as the party ended on a note of heartfelt friendship and good will. I had planned the party, but my guests were so thoroughly in the mood I'd hoped for that by the end of the evening it was their party too. And that's the way it should be.

Mood is what you're aiming for, whether it's Christmas or any other time of year. A party is a form of communication with others—a statement that "I am not alone"—a reinforcement of friendship. A sense of mutual support makes all of us thrive, no matter what our circumstances. I have even given parties in hospital wards! And once I gave a party in a hospital where I myself was at the time a patient.

At seventeen I had just been told that I had a congenital heart ailment which required rare surgery; otherwise I would be dead in a few years. I was feeling far from cheerful, needless to say. I waited in a twelve-bed ward with eleven roommates all of whom were also due for surgery, and each as depressed as I. Every so often a fit of tears would sweep across the room like a storm squall, beginning at the first bed and continuing until every one of us was involved. Why, it's contagious, I thought! And that gave me my idea: why not have a party, then and there—and get us all into a positive mood?

My resources were a bit limited in such a situation. Still, I made do with what was available—a cardinal rule for the Party Girl. There were three other young women in the ward who, like myself, were not completely incapacitated, I enlisted their help, and we conspired with the dietician to serve strawberry ice cream that afternoon to all the patients in our ward. Then, while the others savored this treat, my helpers and I put on a fashion show, modeling hospital gowns!

"They're terribly versatile," I said, in my best fashion-show voice, as I paraded around a make-believe runway to the tune of imaginary violins. "See how chic this little number is, tied up at the sides? Reversible, too . . . and look, they're air-conditioned! It's absolutely the latest thing in California fashions, and Paris is simply mad with envy!"

Our audience was laughing, every one of them, when

83

the nursing supervisor came in to see what was going on —and stayed to join in the laughter herself. I've given a lot of parties since that day, but none of them has meant more to me than that spur-of-the-moment effort on one of the worst days of my life.

I thought that would be my first and last hospital party, but I gave another one some years later—this time in honor of Louis Lurie of San Francisco. Mr. Lurie had managed to break his leg walking out of the Mark Hopkins Hotel, which he happens to own, along with quite a bit of other choice real estate. He was seventy-eight, eligible for Medicare—which had gone into effect only a month before the accident. He wasn't the first Medicare patient at the hospital, but he was the first millionaire who decided to let Medicare foot the bills. So I planned a Medicare party to celebrate this notable event.

News of our little gathering managed to spread, and the first Medicare party was covered by photographers and other representatives of the press. My friends and I came to the party dressed in nurse's uniforms and surgeons' gowns, except that I wore a Richard Tam evening gown under my uniform, since I came directly to the hospital from a television appearance. I was able to provide a floor show of sorts, stripping down to my gold lamé during the party! We brought food and drink with us, and a good deal of reading material for entertainment—stacks and stacks of pamphlets for Mr. Lurie, all about the benefits of Medicare. He loved it—and of course so did the hospital staff, because we were helping to keep their number one patient happy.

Speaking of life-and-death matters, remember the year the Giants *almost* won the pennant? It was so close that the city of San Francisco was like a morgue when the news finally arrived that our heroes had lost to those unmentionable Los Angeles Dodgers. And I had already made elaborate plans for a Victory Celebration. Not only that, but a fine gin company had offered to supply all the liquor I needed; all I had to do was plan the party, invite the guests, and act as hostess.

I consulted the company and we hastily revised all plans. Other victory celebrations had been canceled, but we decided to give a wake instead. After all, why cut ourselves out of a party? Telegrams were sent to the invitation list: "Black crêpe for your arm . . . and a nice cold dry martini to cry into." I decorated a room at the Fairmont Hotel with huge pictures of baseballs, with sad tear-stained faces painted on them. Orange and black streamers were appropriate (the Giants' colors), and naturally we supplied black crying towels to our guests along with the martinis, and black crêpe armbands. Nostalgically, we dined on hot dogs and ballpark peanuts-in-their-shells, reminiscing about the good old days earlier in the season, and predicting doom for the Dodgers the following year. It turned out to be a surprisingly gay party.

On several occasions liquor firms have been happy to supply all the drinks I needed for rather large parties. Reason: public relations, directly beneficial to their own pocketbooks. Retailers and manufacturers were anxious to promote their products and build good will in the community, and they can be very helpful to the experienced hostess in this way. One caution, though. If you want help with a party, work out the details of it in good time, and ask your local firm early for consideration. Most of these firms have a strict budget for such publicity items, which they must follow carefully.

In a lighthearted mood recently, I decided to give a

False Eyelash Party for my lady friends. I consulted a cosmetic firm about my idea, and they cooperated with me in every detail. An expert was sent over to my apartment, to give us instructions and beauty treatments while we all sipped champagne. It was very silly and gay, and everyone went home looking like a movie queen.

Childrens' parties can have themes too. If you are on your own and childless, you might give a party for your friends' children. Kids between the ages of about eight and thirteen are the most delightful guests in the world.

If it's a rainy day, give your favorite little girls a Grownup Tea Party. Get out your old clothes, borrow enough high heels to go around, and have plenty of gloves and hats on hand. Help the little girls get all dressed up, and then serve them in style, with your best china, silver and linen. Tiny bouquets on the table, little cakes and cookies—the works. They'll fall into the spirit of the thing, and their manners will be delicious to observe.

Children love to act, so if you're not up to writing a full-length play for them clip interesting stories out of magazines and newspapers and let them make up skits to fit the material. Headlines such as "Boy Rescued from Lion's Cage" or "Astronauts Walk in Space" can keep them happy for hours. It's good clean fun, provided *you* do the clipping ahead of time. "Hippie Strip Party" or "Hell's Angels to Lecture on Wife-Swapping" might lead to complications you hadn't anticipated.

The simplest arrangements are the best for kids—as long as you have some definite activity planned, something they don't ordinarily do every day. With a minimum of expense and effort you can give a Watermelon Party they will never forget. Just buy some big, juicy watermelons and put them in tubs of ice outdoors. Tell your guests to wear their bathing suits, show them the watermelons, and tell them to go to it. Keep an eye on the action, though, because pretty soon they'll be spitting seeds and throwing rinds all over the place. Separate the contestants only when disaster seems inevitable; it's all part of the game. When the party's over, just hose down your guests, wrap them in towels and deliver them to their parents, ready for a good night's sleep.

That's about as simple as a party can get, but the fact is that when you are entertaining for the most sophisticated adults many of the same basic principles apply. People enjoy the sense that something unusual has been arranged just for them, they like the refreshments to be simple and delicious, and appreciate a chance to do something that is fun. It helps to loosen them up if something novel in the way of costume is the order of the day. If it's considered a bore in your circles for grownups to sit around in the backyard spitting watermelon seeds, how about giving a Bal en Costume de Cinéma, instead?

I organized a party like this a few years ago during the San Francisco International Film Festival, and it was a great success. Many of our guests were celebrities visiting the city for the festival, and I've never seen guests respond so enthusiastically to the idea of coming to a party in costume. They outdid themselves that night, and the results were truly spectacular.

I carried out my theme down to the last detail. Invitations were printed as theatre tickets. Klieg lights were stationed at the host's Pacific Heights mansion, and a great gathering of youngsters from the neighborhood was on hand to collect the autographs of the "stars." Each guest was asked to dress as his favorite film personality. One couple, playing Antony and Cleopatra, stirred up a storm as they arrived from a few blocks away with four bearers in loincloths carrying Elizabeth Taylor's double on an elegant platform. Another foursome, done up like the Beatles with mop wigs and Mod outfits, brought their own children to make sure there would be enough whooping on the sidelines as they made their entry, but of course that proved unnecessary. I arranged to have a wet slab of concrete in the sidewalk outside the house, so guests could immortalize their hand- and footprints, as the stars do in front of Grauman's Chinese Theatre in Hollywood. Newspaper photographers covering the event loved this gag, especially when "Mae West" arrived and got trapped in the wet cement. She was finally freed, amid cheers from all the bystanders.

Inside the house, we created a Hollywood atmosphere, with director's chairs placed around the rooms and huge Oscar-like statuettes borrowed from a local trophy firm. An ice carving of an Oscar stood on the buffet table, and we had a butler in livery who announced the names of the "stars" as they arrived. The orchestra played tunes from various films, and at midnight stopped for a skit in which our guests had a chance to laugh at themselves, in the form of a gossip-columnist-style "exposé." They seemed to enjoy it—at least no lawsuits were filed the following day.

Looking back, I think my favorite party of all, though, was that Carnaby Street bash I mentioned earlier. I love thinking about it, not only because it was such an outstanding success but because that was the night I decided to write this book.

I went all-out for that party, and Carnaby Street itself was not more madly Mod than my apartment when I finished decorating. Again I borrowed the flat upstairs so as to have plenty of space for a large crowd, and the upper rooms became a nightclub, with music by a young rock-and-roll group. I christened them the Liverpool Four, and they liked the name so much they have continued to use it professionally. The walls were covered with Mod drawings in fluorescent colors, and we used "black lighting" to pick up the colors and make them glow. Downstairs, I moved all of my furniture into one of the bedrooms except for a sectional sofa, which I covered in a red and orange print. The same fabric was used to cover one of the walls in the living room.

Guests matched my efforts with really marvelous costumes. There were turtle-necked shirts, miniskirts, and sensational little shifts whipped up by some of the cleverest dressmakers in town (this was when the Mod theme was so new you couldn't find your costume "on the rack"). One man was a superb Edwardian dandy, in a suit he borrowed from his tailor! My small bar was turned into a Beatles Room, with blown-up photographs of the boys from Liverpool. As for the food, I decided we should have English pub-style fare, so I scouted around for a restaurant that would cater it for me. I decided to have a few try-outs on the pork pies and pickled eels, and this turned out to be a very good idea indeed. We discovered, among other things, that "fish 'n chips" tastes terrible unless it's really hot. I found a place which would deliver theirs, wrapped in English newspapers, hot from the stove, and they agreed to keep me supplied all evening by taxi. Before the evening was over they had sent twenty-five batches of food, and I'd had one of the most hilarious experiences of my hostess career. . . .

The delivery boy was a very pleasant-faced, serious young thing, who seemed absolutely dazzled by my two hundred Mod-costumed guests and me in my cut-velvet pantsuit. On the first trip he shyly asked me for a drink, and I said of course he could. Well, as it turned out that wasn't such a good idea. The next time he marched right up and got one for himself. And as I said, the restaurant sent him over to the party twenty-five times. I don't really know how many times he went to the bar, but I did notice that he carried a little black notebook and kept writing in it. "What are you doing?" I asked him finally. "Oh, I'm just writing a book about parties," he said, and vanished into the night to make another trip.

Much later the shy young man was forgotten, and I was saying goodbye to the last of my guests. My friend Marilyn and I made the rounds of the apartment, doing all the little things a hostess should never leave to the help, or to chance. We snuffed out the candles, checked behind the curtains and under sofa cushions for lighted cigarettes, emptied the ashtrays one last time, made sure the back door was locked—and put the front door back on its hinges. Then Marilyn went into the bedroom to get her coat, and I heard her let out a terrific scream. I rushed in after her, but she had already stopped screaming and begun to laugh. There was little Mr. Fish 'n Chips, passed out in the middle of my soft pink bed, with a cherubic smile on his face and his little notebook still clutched in his hand.

"Well, Pat," said Marilyn, when she had recovered, "I guess *you're* going to have to write that book."

And so I did.

CHAPTER SIX

Cinderella Was a Fink

Cinderella was no heroine. She knew perfectly well there was going to be a ball, but what did she do about it? She sat in the corner covered with ashes and soot, feeling sorry for herself. She didn't make one single attempt to improve her situation, or to get herself ready for the big event. Cinderella was a fink.

If you sit moping in your corner like Cinderella, hoping for your fairy godmother to come rescue you, you're going to have an awfully long wait. It's a much better idea to take a good long look at yourself instead, and see what you can do in the way of self-help.

Ask yourself a few important questions first:

1. Do you feel that everyone else is getting the breaks?
2. Do you criticize but resent criticism?
3. If you lose your job, your man or your friend, is it always the other person's fault?
4. Are you fearful and anxious without real cause?
5. Do you mind other people's business?
6. Do you feel that no good will ever come of anything?

If you answer yes to any of these questions, you need personality first aid. Professional help is indicated, of course, if your problem in any of these areas is severe. But there's a great deal a girl can do for herself if she's willing to face her difficulties with honesty, and take a constructive point of view about her life. And in the long run, even with professional help, *it depends on you.*

Take stock of yourself. Personality first aid begins with the development of self-respect, one step at a time. Ask yourself: what have I got to offer to the world which is uniquely *me?* How can I contribute my time, my thoughts and my energies to others in a way that will be creative and meaningful? No one deserves happiness as a natural right. We have to earn it, and giving to others is the best way to begin.

Then take a few solemn vows to get yourself started in new directions:

Never criticize unless you are prepared to accept criticism yourself. Avoid gossip at all times; invariably it will come back to haunt you. If you have constructive criticism to make, offer it to the person concerned; don't say it behind his or her back.

Stop blaming others when things go wrong. Stand aside and carefully consider, with as much objectivity as possible, every step you made and every word you said. If you decide it was your fault, be willing to accept the blame. It's often said that we learn more from our mistakes than from our triumphs; but you can't learn from your mistakes unless you admit them. Admit it when you don't know all the answers—allow yourself the luxury of being human! A wise old lady I know once remarked about a self-righteous young committeewoman in the community, "The trouble with Beverly is, she has yet to make her first mistake." Poor Beverly!

Most of our fears are rooted in insecurity. A girl who doesn't have a good opinion of herself is afraid of losing her job, afraid of being left out in social gatherings, and she certainly isn't very good hostess material. She slops around the house in a dirty bathrobe and goes to work in clothes held together by safety pins. She thinks it doesn't matter what *she* looks like. The other girls have the pretty eyes, the lustrous hair and the slender figures rounded in all the right places. She's out of luck, she thinks—so she turns herself into a total slob.

A girl like this should realize that the natural endowments are only a fraction of the secret of being beautiful. Women who are positively ugly can be sexy, charming, fascinating and distinguished—and, with clever grooming, a pleasure to behold. The most-admired faces we see on the screen today are those with offbeat looks and individual personality. There is a reason for this, I think. In a world of computers and lost identities we seize upon the looks which indicate originality of mind and spirit. Pretty-faced people are a bore; we want to see somebody who looks like a real person. Never has the field been so wide open as it is these days, for women who were not blessed with conventional beauty.

The girl who doesn't like her looks or herself takes an abnormal interest in other people's lives. She's a snooper who can't mind her own business, because in her own opinion she has no business to mind. She's a pessimist, and sees disaster around every corner. It always rains on Sunday if you're planning a picnic—so why bother? Well, you miss out on an awful lot of picnics that way!

Because you're a woman, your personal appearance is extremely important to your psyche. A terrible hairdo or ten pounds in the wrong spot can turn you into a grouch. But oh, how gorgeous the world looks when you're looking at it from under the brim of a marvelous new hat! Rose-colored glasses were never like this. So don't play Cinderella. Take stock of your basic equipment, decide what you have to work with, and see what you can do with it. This means, first of all, your body: weight, posture, figure, hair, complexion, grace of movement, voice tone, everything down to the last detail. Prepare yourself to feel beautiful, because the way you feel about yourself can change your life.

Nothing is more important to your appearance than weight and posture, so here's a chart for you to use, keeping track of my suggested program of diet and exercise. Let's begin on it *now*. If you make a real effort, you'll be amazed at the results.

A diet that I have tried and like very much is the one that Dr. Rudolf E. Noble, M.D., Ph.D., San Francisco's noted authority on obesity and author of the *Calorie Game*, has formulated. He calls it "The Thinking Girl's Diet." Here are some of his comments regarding weight reduction:

> Before embarking on a specific diet it is best to have some knowledge of the interrelationship between calorie counting and weight loss. The National Research Council tells us that a woman between the ages of eighteen to thirty-five, of average height and weight, in good health and leading a moderately active life, requires 2,100 calories a day to maintain her weight. Weight loss comes about when you have taken in less calories a day than your body needs to sustain your existing weight. Every time you achieve a caloric deficit of 3,500 calories you will lose a pound of weight. Therefore, if you need 2,100 calories a day to maintain your weight and you go on a 1,200-calorie diet a day, you will lose about two pounds a week or eight pounds in a month.

Your diet should include representatives from the dairy, meat, vegetable, fruit and wheat groups. You should use a calorie counter and keep daily track of your calories. Here is a one-week well-balanced 1,200-calorie diet. You are to avoid extra foods and in-between-meal snacks for they will mean extra calories. Syrup, sugar, oils, extra fats or larger servings of food would also mean extra calories. Coffee or tea, black or with low calorie sweeteners may be used as desired. Green salads should be made of lettuce, tomatoes, and radishes, and you should use only vinegar or "low-calorie" dressing. Any woman staying on a prolonged weight-reducing program should see her physician to make sure that the chosen diet is the correct one for her. Your physician may want to give you some vitamin and mineral supplementation.

YOUR MEASURE OF SUCCESS

Name:_____

Date: _____

	Start	Ideal	Finish
Height			
Weight			
Bust			
Waist			
Upper Hip			
Center Hip			
Lower Hip			
Thigh			
Above Knee			
Calf			
Ankle			

Diet:_____

Exercise:_____

1. Do you stand up straight? _____
2. Are you ashamed of your weight? _____
3. Do you subscribe to at least one "common-sense" fashion magazine? _____
4. Do you walk in a graceful manner? _____
5. Do you plop into chairs helter-skelter? _____
6. Do you chew gum in public? _____
7. Do you know what colors look best on you? _____
8. Are you held together with safety pins? _____
9. Does your slip show—ever? _____
10. Do you experiment with ways to wear your hair? _____
11. Does your make-up blend with your dress color? _____
12. Do you dress with flair? _____
13. Do you ever analyze yourself in a three-way mirror? _____
14. Are you in a one-lipstick-a-year rut? _____
15. Are you a catch-your-reflection girl? _____
16. Do you have a perfume identity? _____
17. Do you wear chipped nail polish? _____
18. Do you defuzz your legs and underarms regularly? _____
19. Do you use a deodorant daily? _____
20. Do you think only the rich can be chic? _____
21. Do you wear "sets" of jewelry? _____
22. Are you a good listener? _____
23. Are you a chronic complainer? _____
24. Do you dress in the same vein as everyone around you? _____
25. Do you count your calories? _____
26. Do you shampoo your hair *before* it gets dirty? _____

27. Do you enter a room gracefully? _____
28. Do you overdress? _____
29. Do your clothes have a current silhouette? _____
30. Are your white touches always white? _____
31. Do you try to wear clothing "one more time" before cleaning? _____
32. Would your clothes closet stand inspection right now? _____
33. Do you have a negative attitude? _____
34. Do you wear dress shields? _____
35. Do you ever leave make-up on overnight? _____
36. Do you know your special assets? _____
37. Are you a hair-puller or hand-wringer? _____
38. Do you expect results from "self-improvement efforts" overnight? _____
39. Do you greet people with a positive statement? _____
40. Are you considerate of others? _____
41. Are you petty? _____
42. Are you more concerned with what your neighbor is doing, than with what *you* are doing? _____
43. Do you make others feel important? _____
44. Do you have a positive attitude? _____
45. Do you possess the qualities you like in others? _____
46. Do you have a happy voice? _____
47. Do you criticize others in an effort to build up your own image? _____
48. Do you make an effort to remember and recognize people? _____
49. Do you care enough about your appearance, your husband, your job to devote the time and effort to become a person you would admire?

"The Thinking Girl's Diet"

	MONDAY	TUESDAY	WEDNESDAY
Breakfast	Orange juice (small glass) 1 Egg (boiled) 1 Slice toast (buttered) Coffee or tea	Grapefruit (½ small) 1 Egg (fried) Cereal, dry (¾ cup with 1 cup skim milk) Coffee or tea	Orange juice (small glass) 1 Egg (boiled) 1 Slice toast (buttered) Coffee or tea
Lunch	Clear broth Hamburger patty (4 oz.) Green salad Skim milk or buttermilk (1 glass) Coffee or tea	Bouillon (fat-free) Roast beef (4 oz.) Green salad Diet cola Coffee or tea	Clear broth Hamburger patty (4 oz.) Green salad Skim milk or buttermilk (1 glass) Coffee or tea
Dinner	Steak (4 oz.) Stewed carrots (½ cup) Potato, boiled (1 small) Green salad Skim milk or buttermilk (1 glass) Apple (1 small) Coffee or tea	Chicken, broiled, 6 oz. Green peas (½ cup) Rice, cooked (½ cup) Green salad Skim milk or buttermilk (1 glass) Pear (1 small) Coffee or tea	Steak (4 oz.) Stewed carrots (½ cup) Potato, boiled (1 small) Green salad Skim milk or buttermilk (1 glass) Apple (1 small) Coffee or tea

Dr. Rudolf Noble's "Two-Pound-a-Week Diet" for the Working Girl*

THURSDAY	FRIDAY	SATURDAY	SUNDAY
Grapefruit (½ small) 1 Egg (fried) Cereal, dry (¾ cup with 1 cup skim milk) Coffee or tea	Orange juice (small glass) 1 Egg (boiled) 1 Slice toast (buttered) Coffee or tea	Grapefruit (½ small) 1 Egg (fried) Cereal, dry (¾ cup with 1 cup skim milk) Coffee or tea	**Brunch** Champagne (4 oz.) Cheese omelette Chicken livers (2 oz.) Blueberry muffln (1) Honeydew melon (¼) Coffee or tea
Bouillon (fat-free) Roast beef (4 oz.) Green salad Diet cola Coffee or tea	Clear broth Hamburger patty (4 oz.) Green salad Skim milk or buttermilk (1 glass) Coffee or tea	Bouillon (fat-free) Roast beef (4 oz.) Green salad Diet cola Coffee or tea	
Chicken, broiled, 6 oz. Green peas (½ cup) Rice, cooked (½ cup) Green salad Skim milk or buttermilk (1 glass) Pear (1 small) Coffee or tea	Filet of sole 6 oz., broiled Squash (½ cup) Roll (1) Green salad Skim milk or buttermilk (1 glass) Pineapple (½ cup) Coffee or tea	Steak (4 oz.) Stewed carrots (½ cup) Potato, boiled (1 small) Green salad Skim milk or buttermilk (1 glass) Apple (1 small) Coffee or tea	Veal (4 oz.) sautéed Squash (½ cup) Bread (1 small) Green salad Ice cream (½ scoop) Coffee or tea

*A 1,200-calorie/day diet designed for a young woman of average height, weight, activity, in good health and requiring 2,100 calories a day to maintain her weight (see earlier in chapter).

Now you are nine pounds thinner—providing, of course, you've been faithful to the diet. You know enough not to sneak double malteds on the side, but be sure not to sneak peanuts or peppermints either. Every snack you sneak is a calorie trap. You've been on the wagon too, I'm sorry to say. A diet simply won't work if you augment it with alcohol; and it's bad for your psyche anyway to drink during a diet, because it tends to make you lose your will-power. If you crave a cocktail while dieting, try fooling yourself with substitutes: hot coffee, tea or consommé, sipped slowly, and the tranquilizing thought of how slim and lovely you're going to be very soon.

If you're not on a specific diet, remember these pointers to keep your weight down:

1. Drink buttermilk or skim milk, and low-calorie soft drinks.
2. No sugar or cream in beverages.
3. Fruit for dessert, and stay away from pastries of all kinds.
4. Lemon juice or vinegar, on salads.
5. Eat only one starch; choose between potatoes, bread, rice or noodles.
6. Limit the size of portions—and no seconds!

Men may not like fat women, but they do like curves in the right places, so girls who are underweight have a problem too. If nervousness is seriously affecting your appetite, by all means consult a doctor. But if it's just a matter of poor eating habits, carelessness and haste, tell yourself that weight-gain is project number one on your list, beginning today. Hungry or not, stow away three meals a day, and force yourself to eat fattening snacks at bedtime.

Breakfast for gainers should include fruit or juice, one-half cup of cereal with sugar and cream, one egg, at least one slice of bread with one-half tablespoon of butter and a glass of whole milk. For lunch have creamed soup, a sandwich, dessert of cake or pie, and coffee with cream and sugar. Dinner should begin with either fruit, juice or soup, and include meat, potato, green vegetable with butter, salad, bread and butter, and a hearty dessert.

If you gag at the thought of between-meal snacks after all this, try drinking a can or two of eggnog just before you go to sleep. This adds considerably to your daily caloric intake, quite painlessly, and without destroying what is left of your appetite for regular meals. The best time to gain weight is in the evening—and this is something the dieters should keep in mind too. If you're lumpy around the middle, keep away from the kitchen after dinnertime. Make yourself a cup of cocoa or coffee just before retiring, if you simply can't get to sleep without a snack. Sing yourself a lullaby, suck your thumb if necessary, but *don't eat!*

ALL ABOUT EXERCISE. Achieving the right weight is a great accomplishment, but it's not enough. Your body must be firm and lithe and sure of itself. Unless you have unlimited time and ability to play tennis and golf, to ride and swim, you will have to exercise regularly in order to keep fit. Don't feel sorry for yourself, and don't get self-conscious about it. When you exercise for beauty, you're joining a popular international club, really—you're doing what all the smartest, most glamorous women in the world do today. Those with unlimited means can be found at the gym in their private clubs, attending daily exercise sessions. Others go to classes at the YWCA for regular workouts, or join the moderately priced health clubs that are in most cities. Yoga classes are booming in popularity, and they are well worth your consideration. They teach you mental discipline along with body control, and give you a well-integrated philosophy of life which helps you to stay beautiful, as you grow older. Judo is a marvelous discipline too, and if you are *very* attractive, you might find it quite useful at times. It teaches you, among other things, how to throw a man across a room without breaking him into little pieces.

If you can't afford lessons of any sort, you can still walk, run and climb stairs—and you can follow a do-it-yourself exercise routine at home. Once you have chosen your discipline, stick to it, each day at a certain time, preferably in the morning. Don't decide to skip it today because you were out partying till 3 A.M., or working late. Exercise will help revive your tired muscles, and improved circulation will tend to erase the circles under your eyes. It's a good idea to have some sort of exercise suit to slip into. It makes the whole thing more businesslike. Some girls exercise to music—I know one who dances around her apartment every morning to a Trini Lopez LP, and emerges looking marvelous.

Most of us, I guess, are pretty lazy, and that's why I've chosen Isometrics, over so-called effortless exercise, to recommend here. It's the easiest and simplest way of all to control those curves. In this system a muscle is held in static (acting as a weight but not moving) contraction for not more than six seconds. The first three weeks of these exercises, you hold the contraction for not more than six seconds. Maintain normal breathing during the exercise, and don't think it's necessary to do them more than once daily. The benefits would be negligible.

The underlying principles of isometric exercise were discovered in the 1920s, when scientists found that one leg of a frog grew definitely stronger when tied down over a period of time. Later on, doctors applied this observation to the improvement of the human body. Normal, known as "isotonic," exercise strengthens a muscle by moving it. Isometric exercise does not move the muscle—you perform the exercises against an immovable, often imaginary object. Here are isometric exercises for all parts of the body:

A. Waist. Standing with chin and chest high, draw in stomach muscles and contract, pulling in stomach muscles tighter and tighter until you feel as if your stomach is touching your spine.

B. Breast Developer. Interlock fingers with palms pressed together, hands and elbows the same level, and push strongly against each palm. Pressure is increased until a little quiver is felt.

C. Neck Slimmer. Lock fingers together (both hands), place behind head. Try to push head forward with your hands while exerting a backward force with head and neck. Hold. Do same with hands on forehead while resisting with head and neck. Hold. Now push against right side of head with right palm. Repeat left side. Hold.

D. Forearm Slimming. Bend arm at elbow. Clench fingers into fist and grip and squeeze. Hold.

E. Calf and Thigh Slimming. Stand erect, reach up with both hands, rising up on toes and tightening the thigh and calf. Hold.

F. Firming the Thigh. Bend your knee, raise leg as you stand on ball of opposite foot. Concentrate on upper part of the leg. Contract and hold.

G. Calf slimming. While sitting, raise your right leg,

bending at the knee. Lace fingers of both hands below your knee and pull toward your body. Now resist with muscles of calf contracted. Hold.

THE BEAUTY ROUTINE. The late Lady Mendl said she felt she owed it to the world to look her best because everybody else had to look at her. Well, remember—people have to look at you too. It's not just a kindness to yourself, or a matter of mere vanity, when you make an effort to be attractive and well-groomed. You're paying a compliment to everyone around you, because you're saying, in effect, "I care enough about you to care for myself."

Don't excuse yourself on the grounds that you haven't time for a beauty routine! It's like saying you haven't time to live. Every woman wants to live in a beautiful house; but sometimes we forget that our bodies are the houses *we* live in, from the moment we are born until we die. A lovely complexion is far more important to a woman, in the long run, than a set of freshly waxed floors, or an apartment redone by the best decorator in town. So care for your body *first*, then turn to the other chores and ambitions in your life.

Be regular, above all, in the care of your skin. Set up a daily program for cleansing, toning, moisturizing and lubrication. Each morning and night, you should cleanse your face and neck carefully with a cream or liquid skin-cleanser, then tone with a skin-freshener. Moisturize during the day, lubricate the eye and throat areas at night, and put on a night cream faithfully. The clever new creams on the market are designed to penetrate your skin without leaving a gooey mask on the surface, so you can look quite civilized day and night while you are guarding the health of your skin. The old cartoon image of the dumpy frau in iron curlers with lard smeared all over her face is definitely a thing of the past!

In betweentimes, you'll have your various makeup routines, and you should practise them until your hand is as deft as a magician's. Judging by some of the magazine articles I've read, a great many girls are spending too much time dabbing at their faces with dozens of different cosmetic products, and the results, are not always very pleasant to look at. Simplicity in all things should be your watchword. Clean out your bathroom cabinet and your dressing-table drawers first of all if you want to make yourself into a real beauty, and keep only the items which have proved their worth for *you*. The basis of all beauty is self-confidence and radiant good health. What you add to this in the way of makeup should be carefully and deliberately planned to heighten your own natural and individual charm. *Don't be Brand X!* Be yourself.

During the day, you may choose to wear very little makeup, depending on the type of job you have. A skillful touch-up of the eyes, a moisturizer and lip gloss (five minutes, at most) are all that's needed for some girls. In general, it's best to do the minimum paint job during the day, and then let yourself go a bit at the dressing-table when you're preparing for an evening appearance under artificial light. Evening makeup, too, depends ultimately upon the bloom of health and good spirits—but it should be *fun*, and it can be as daring as you like. After all, you're not trying to look like a member in good standing of the Girl Scouts of America when you go to a cocktail party.

Operation Preparation: The Forty-minute Miracle. It's really possible—new energy, new face, new woman, all in forty minutes' time. Here's how I do it: I dash into the house, *not* stopping to chat or read the paper, and start the bath running as I take off my clothes. Put up my hair fast, in huge rollers, and dust lightly with spray. Begin working on my face and throat (upward and outward strokes, of course) with my favorite brand of liquid cleanser, pour a generous helping of bath oil into the tub with the other hand, and climb into the tub with cleanser still on face. Now soak blissfully for five full minutes. Take cleanser off with a soft cloth (tissue not so good for this, it has wood fibres in it) and wash with a deliciously creamy soap. Rinse thoroughly with warm water, then a splash of cold. Fifteen minutes are gone, and it's time to get out of the tub.

I wrap luxuriously in a huge "bath sheet," and after drying smooth on a moisturizing cream from head to toe. This not only serves as a moisturizer, but also protects facial skin, under makeup to follow. The scene now shifts to the bedroom, where I lie face down on a slantboard for five minutes, relaxing completely. Already I'm beginning to feel alive again!

Twenty-five minutes have passed, and I spend the remaining fifteen of the "miracle" at the dressing table. Mine is encircled with lights, so I can really see what I'm doing; if you don't put on makeup in a strong light you're fooling yourself. And use a magnifying mirror too; it's a great help with the finer details.

Tonight I'm going to paint the town a bit, so I begin with my face. Liquid foundation first, in two shades, which I blend carefully for contouring, playing as if with light and shadow. Foundation goes on throat and neck, as well as face, to avoid a mask-like look in the finished production.

Now for the eyebrows, and let me say frankly that

most women mess them up. *Don't* pluck any more than absolutely necessary! That thin, hard look went out with the thirties, and it never should have come in to begin with. It looks cheap and awful. *Don't* draw a hard, dark line with an eyebrow pencil, or fill it in till it looks pasted on. Your eyelashes can look "borrowed" if you like, but your eyebrows should always look like your own. Choose a pencil in a soft color congenial to your own coloring, and apply it in tiny, hairlike strokes. Brush gently (I usually use an eyebrow brush) to remove excess, and don't let the brow droop below the corner of the eyes; a downward line is an aging line.

Now for eye shadow. I prefer to use a cream stick shadow, first in a white tone and over that a beige shadow, smoothed out to the edge of the brow. Mascara on upper lashes only—but tonight I'm wearing my mink eyelashes, so we skip that, apply the falsies, and draw a fine line over the edge where it meets the eyelid, with cake eyeliner—brown for me.

Never wear false eyelashes the way they come from the store—you'll look like Minnie Mouse. They have to be trimmed, in an irregular, feathered manner, shorter in the center and swooping out at the edges.

Now a touch of cream rouge on the cheekbones, blended to the hairline, and then soft honey-colored rouge applied with a sable brush, all over my face, neck and throat to heighten a natural suntan. I outline my lips with a lipstick brush, fill in with a soft pink lipstick, and finally cover the lips with a slick of pale coral. Never powder the lips; they should be fresh and shining.

One last touch is indispensable. I spray my entire body with one of my very favorite, subtle and terribly expensive perfumes that I love. An old beau once had the bright idea of pouring a whole bottle of it over my head, and I've been addicted ever since. But I think every woman in the world should have her own favorite perfume, and use it lavishly. It's expensive, I know, but if she economizes on everything else in life, a woman should see to it that she smells heavenly. And if she smells good enough, sooner or later she's going to find a man who is just dying to go out and buy the stuff for her.

Five minutes left, and I spend them brushing my hair, using a natural-bristle brush. Keep back-combing to a minimum—it causes hair-breaking and splitting. And very little spray after the comb-out, please! A woman should be soft and touchable.

So now it's time to get dressed—and for me those forty minutes have worked a miracle. I'm rested and refreshed, and I know I'm going to look my best this evening. It does take longer, of course, if you want to add a hairpiece, or sprinkle yourself here and there with gold dust, or what-not. But not much, if you've spent a few evenings home alone, practising these arts, as you should.

PRETTY HANDS AND FEET. It's impossible to play hostess successfully if you have to sit on your hands. So make sure you don't need to—keep them as pretty as possible at all times. Mostly it's a matter of grooming, but you might give some thought too to the type of gestures you make. Watch yourself in a mirror sometime, and then study pictures of people who are expert with their hands —such as the little Balinese dancers whose every finger-movement is so utterly entrancing. Do you nervously twist your rings and pluck at your coiffure when you are in a social situation? Try to make yourself conscious of it, so that you can improve your habits. Choose several attractive positions of repose for your hands, and practise them. It is amazing how much body control helps to control your moods. You will *feel* more relaxed with people, actually, if you keep your physical movements smooth and graceful. The outer self is a positive influence upon the inner you.

Few working girls can afford regular manicures, but you can achieve fine results at home by following these simple rules.

Once a week:

1. Remove polish from nails.
2. File with a diamond nail file held in a slanting position. Make oval-shaped nails, filing toward center.
3. Massage cream into nail and over first finger joint.
4. Soak hand in mild-soapy water.
5. Apply cuticle remover and remove excess cuticle.
6. When nail is dry and clean, apply base coat.
7. Apply pale colored polish in long, even strokes, remove a hairline from the tip of the nail to prevent chipping. Allow polish to dry, and repeat.

This routine should take you about half an hour. During the week give extra care to your nails and hands by applying hand creams and cuticle creams regularly. You should have cream or lotion beside each sink in your house, including the kitchen sink, and carry packets of lotion in your purse at all times, to use after each handwashing. If your job prohibits colored polish, use at least the base coat, to protect your nails. For problem nails try a package of pure gelatine once a day, and use white iodine on the nail base in the evening. In ninety days you will have strong healthy nails.

Be kind to your feet! You've got to stand on them, and

other people have to look at them. Give yourself a pedicure the same way you did the manicure, except that you should cut toenails straight across. Use polish on your toenails, and nail cream for strengthening and cuticle-softening. For calluses, use cuticle remover or pumice stone, followed by a soothing antiseptic—and buy yourself shoes that fit. Always perfume your feet before a party. The reason is obvious: some nice man might want to kiss them, and you had better be prepared.

A few more grooming suggestions before we go on to your wardrobe. Your smile is twice as lovely if your teeth look good, so keep them in healthy condition with regular visits to the dentist and regular brushing. Experiment with deodorants and be a faithful user of the one which works best for you. Keep your underarms and legs defuzzed, and if you have a serious problem about unwanted hair, follow a physician's advice. Whatever your mirror tells you, pay attention! Circles under the eyes, for example, are a signal for you to get more rest—so don't pretend to yourself that they aren't there, and don't think it's enough to cover them up with "white makeup base." Take good care of yourself. You'll be glad you did.

YOUR WARDROBE AND YOU. Loving pretty clothes is part of being a woman. Clothes are our second skins, our fine plumage. When we arrange our feathers and veils just so, we're doing what comes naturally to females of every species. Unfortunately, good taste and discrimination don't come to us as naturally. It takes time, work and study for a woman to achieve the right sort of wardrobe for her own personality and the life she leads.

I was given an unforgettable lesson on the subject when I was still in grade school back in Oklahoma. I was one of three children selected as tops in an elocution contest, and all the parents and friends were invited to attend the final event in the school auditorium. It was a grand occasion, of course, and I wanted to dress up for it. Like most little girls, I thought pink taffeta with lots of frills and furbelows was the ultimate in chic. I was utterly crushed when the ladies of the church made me an outfit of blue-and-white-checked gingham, with matching panties, and my parents took me to the drug store and bought red grograin ribbons to tie up my pigtails.

I suffered the pangs of martyrdom when I appeared in this before a sea of faces in the auditorium. It was too much to bear that they hadn't even let me wear some nice, sleazy little pink silk panties for the occasion, I thought. How could anyone win a contest dressed like this? I stared steadfastly at my brother in the back row, and grimly recited the story of "Little Johnny Squirrel."

Well, I won, and I was sent on to the county contest. "I *won't* wear that dress again," I stormed to my mother. "Patsy Lou, you are making a mistake," my mother replied. "That dress is just right for you. It's very becoming, and it suits the occasion perfectly." Of course she was absolutely right. Pink taffeta would have looked tawdry and hopelessly inappropriate. In the smart little gingham outfit I looked fresh and appealing, simply but imaginatively dressed for the occasion—and surely that *is* chic.

Take stock of your wardrobe now on this basis. Ask yourself whom and what am I dressing *for?* And what is my true personality? Be ruthless. Weed out *all* the clothes that aren't right for you and your life, even if you have to throw out nearly everything you own.

This sounds drastic, and it is, but it's necessary if you're going to make yourself over into a star. You don't have to appear with top billing on stage, in films or TV to be a star—you can be one in your own life, as it is right at this moment. Every piece of clothing you own should say something positive about *you*.

You can profit in more than one way by this operation. In most cities and towns there are shops which sell second-hand clothes for charitable causes. They will give you an estimate of what your clothing is worth, and you can deduct this from your income tax. Luxury items, seldom worn and still in style, but not for *you*, can often be placed with shops which sell secondhand fashions to bargain hunters, and you may raise a little ready cash this way to help with a new wardrobe.

Now you are ready to rebuild. Take it slowly, because you are going to do it *right* this time. Tend to the necessities before you fool with the frills. Buy yourself something marvelous to wear to work, first of all. Whether you're a housewife, a sales clerk or a movie queen, you spend most of your waking hours in work clothes of one sort or another. *Don't* buy things because you think they will be "serviceable"—buy them because they are madly becoming to you, and wholly appropriate to your specific job situation. "Serviceable" clothes are a bore.

Now buy yourself an absolutely smashing party dress. *Not* the meek little-black-dress you can accessorize so it looks different every time, but something sensational. Would you rather look mediocre three different ways, or unforgettable in the same dress three times in a row? The smartest women in the world buy great clothes, pay high prices for them, and keep on wearing them for years. Buy high fashion, and buy the best you can afford.

I have an ambivalent attitude toward black. Three-quarters of the girls at most cocktail parties are wearing black, and so I like to steer away from it. Still, being blond and generally tanned, black is a good color for me. So I buy a black dress once in a while, but only when it's a real knockout. Why should black be "basic"? That's a holdover from the days when cleaning was a real problem. The coin-operated do-it-yourself dry-cleaning establishments have changed all that. Now a woman's "basic" dress can be any color she chooses. How about basic white? Or pink? Pink is the sexiest color in the world, so do yourself a favor and find out exactly which shade of pink is most becoming to you. Try different color swatches next to your skin, choose the one that turns you on, and make yourself a dress in that shade, or have one made. A woman dressed in the right shade of pink is a woman in full bloom!

Consider next your at-home outfits. You do change when you come home from work, I trust. It's the only sensible way to operate. You save your expensive office clothes this way, and you give yourself a fresh start late in the day by slipping into something comfortable and glamorous. Your first at-home costumes may be simple cotton muumuus; later, when you are well established in your hostess role, you'll want a varied wardrobe of long skirts, dinner gowns, pantsuits and hostess culottes. My own daytime dresses stress elegant simplicity, but I like a flamboyant touch in hostess costumes. I've had my favorite culottes copied in several fabrics, so I can choose from zebra stripes, pink Thai silk, emerald-green velvet, orange-and-pink-striped cotton and pleated sapphire-blue chiffon. I love culottes, because they're so graceful, sexy and feminine. And I've noticed that men love them too, even the ones who swear they hate seeing women in pants.

What if you're home alone—do you say to yourself in this case, "Why bother?" This brings us back to the basic question of self-esteem. You know you'd be ashamed to welcome an unexpected visitor wearing a soiled robe and a headful of rollers. So why be a slob when you're keeping yourself company? You are as important to yourself as a casual visitor might be, and you owe yourself the sense of being pretty, in your own home, on your own time. Rollers are a necessity of life, of course, for most of us. But why not tuck them away under a favorite scarf, after you've washed your hair, and how about wearing a *clean* bathrobe when you're puttering around the boudoir? In the evening a long cotton skirt gives your morale a lift, even if you're just going to read or listen to music by yourself. This helps you develop a habit of mind, an attitude about yourself that's very important in terms of self-respect.

Give yourself a fashion show now and then when you're home alone. Try on all your clothes, and study the successes and failures of your wardrobe. This is a good moment to practise, too, with any new item you own. Learn to move comfortably in it, study the best ways of sitting down and rising gracefully, note the way the fabric behaves as you walk. If you've rehearsed in private with a new garment, you will be sure of yourself when you have an audience. The *movement* of evening clothes is particularly important. When you glide among your guests in diaphanous chiffons and clinging crêpes, you're saying a great deal about yourself without uttering a single word. Sex appeal is difficult to define, but the most astute men I've known have told me it has to do first and foremost with a woman's unspoken attitudes. Your body speaks for you at every moment. And if it's beautifully groomed and dressed with taste and *joie de vivre*, the message is: *I'm glad to be a woman.*

CHAPTER SEVEN

How Far Should
Your Hospitality Go?

As every girl knows, the basic ingredients of any good party are food, liquor and men. Let's discuss them in the usual order here, flipping somewhat lightly over food and drink, and getting on as promptly as possible to the subject which interests us most.

Though, when you think of it, one can't talk about food without talking about men, too. It's a plain fact that the girl whose apartment smells deliciously of fresh-baked bread is far more enticing to most men than the girl who reeks of Shalimar and opens a can of beans for dinner.

The easiest way to become a marvelous cook, of course, is to learn young what good food tastes like. Still, if Mama didn't serve *crêpes farcis et roulés* back home, all is not lost. In the city, you'll have a chance to get around and sample many different kinds of cooking at restaurants and at private homes. Keep your eyes open and every time you taste something outstandingly delicious ask yourself—or better yet, ask the cook—what's in this? How was it prepared? How can I duplicate it, if possible, tomorrow in my own kitchen? Compliment your hostess, and write her

115

a note the next day, asking her to share some of her recipes or kitchen techniques with you. Chances are she'll be delighted to play teacher. If you are in a restaurant, go back to the kitchen and compliment the chef after a particularly fine dinner. He probably *won't* tell you how he did it, but he may drop a few hints, and everything you can learn is bound to help.

Beg, borrow or buy all the good cookbooks you can lay hands on, and study them in your spare time. Set up a regular schedule for yourself: try one new dish each week when you're alone, or with a few close friends who will be tolerant of a first-time failure. I've already mentioned *Mastering the Art of French Cooking*, a book every hostess should own and read from cover to cover. My other favorites are *The Madison Avenue Cookbook*, by Alan Koehler—a great help to ambitious Party Girls who work in a small space with limited equipment—and the book with that marvelous title: *The I Hate to Cook Book*, by Peg Bracken (which I keep on my shelf next to *The Joy of Cooking* for mental balance).

You will find it's absolutely worth the effort: Keep a card file for yourself of recipes you've mooched here and there, with comments about how each dish should be served. Clean out your card file every now and then, because there are fashions in food, as well as clothing and décor. Several years back a Ritz cracker with peanut butter and crumbled bacon, toasted under the broiler, was a perfectly acceptable hors d'oeuvre at an informal cocktail party—but if you came up with a little number like that now, everybody would think you were kidding. Gourmet foods are available at every supermarket these days, fresh, canned or frozen. Take a good look each time you go shopping, and make mental or written notes about new things you want to try.

If food *looks* good, it's actually going to taste better. So remember that the arrangement and service of your food is all-important in successful entertaining. I have a few personal prejudices on this score, which I will pass along here. I love to see plenty of food on a buffet table, but I prefer it served in reasonably small portions. A crowded plate ruins my appetite. Color balance is extremely important to me too, and I think it is to most people, whether or not they are conscious of it. A meal that's all one color (fish, squash and scalloped potatoes) makes me wish I had gone somewhere else for dinner. It's awfully important to offer guests a stimulating variety of tastes, textures and colors in their food, as well as the extra little touches which are the mark of a fine cuisine. By that I don't mean panties on the lamb chops, or paprika faithfully sprinkled on everything that's white, but original and amusing touches of things in good taste, that taste good! For example, fresh watercress, instead of parsley, with the steaks, or paper-thin slices of cucumber, instead of lemon slices, floating in cold summer soups. Fat sprigs of fresh mint are delightful accompaniments to many vegetables as well as fruits—and leaves and flowers from your garden can be used to great advantage, decorating the various plates on your buffet table. If you order a simple breakfast in a cafeteria in the Hawaiian Islands, they're quite likely to decorate your plate with delicate little lavender orchids, and I think that's a fine way to begin any day! Cafeterias on the Mainland have a great deal to learn from their competitors in the fiftieth state. As things stand now you can judge your success as a cook pretty much by this simple little rule: if the food looks or tastes as if it could have been prepared in the cafeteria on the corner, then you're doing it wrong!

It's how your meal looks and how it tastes that counts. Don't worry yourself into a tizzy about where to put the dessert spoons, or what kind of wine glass to use. If your guests are comfortable and everything looks pretty and inviting, that's what matters. You can serve any kind of wine in any kind of glass, if it's good-looking. Centerpieces don't have to be made of expensive cut flowers, even for a formal dinner party. A fine old soup tureen, a pretty bowl of shells, or a simple arrangement of green leaves will suffice. Candles are a must, and if you haven't inherited a ten-branch candelabra you can find plenty of interesting substitutes on the market, or make your own candle holders for practically nothing. One clever young hostess I know simply attaches her candles, by melting a bit of the wax at the bottom, to a number of small saucers; then she fills the saucers with leaves and berries, or wild flowers, gathered for nothing, on her country walks. My own candlesticks were made from old newel posts I discovered in the warehouse of a wrecking company, cleaned up and rubbed with white shoe polish, then with wax. Look around and you'll probably find that you already own a number of odds and ends which would be perfect for table decoration. Almost anything will do except a chamber pot—no plastic flowers either.

Before we turn to the subject of wines and liquors, a few words about the service of your food. The most important point here is that you should think out the entire process very thoroughly well ahead of time. The kind of party you give should depend first of all upon the atmosphere you are able to create for your guests. In other words, don't try to give a formal dinner for thirty if you have an apartment the size of a phone booth. Give a stand-

118

up cocktail party instead, or confine yourself to a seated dinner for six or eight, or a buffet dinner for only a very few more than this. If you seat more than eight at dinner you *must* have someone to help you serve. Otherwise your guests will get frantic and the food will get cold, while you tear around the table like the runner-up at the Roller Derby. For similar reasons, never serve a roast which must be carved at table if you are serving more than four people. The ceremony of carving is charming, at best, only for the first few moments—then it becomes a mess and a bore. Don't carve the roast or the turkey yourself, even if you're a past master at it—at least don't do it where your male guests can see you, or you'll frighten them out of their wits. Always hand the knife to a man, and pretend you don't know how to sharpen it.

When you're giving a buffet avoid drippy foods, and don't serve meat that needs to be cut on the plate. Never serve desserts in bowls which must be balanced on top of plates, or in tippy goblets. Be practical. Buffet dinners are best ended with simple finger foods—fruits, cheese and crackers, petits-fours and the like. Additional sweets, such as little candied fruits or peppermints, may be served on your coffee tray. You may extend your buffet menu to three courses, if you like, by serving soup first, in simple heat proof mugs in the living room, and then inviting your guests to come to the buffet table for the entree; but in general it is wise to serve more than two courses only if you seat your guests and provide them with smooth and inconspicuous service.

LIQUOR AND WINES

Here I think the best thing an inexperienced hostess can do is to go to the neighborhood emporium of liquor and ask the nice man there for advice. If he insists on trying to sell you things you can't afford, go to another store. There are plenty of acceptable brands of hard liquor and wine which needn't wreck the budget if you buy carefully; and it's no disgrace to serve nothing stronger than wine if you can't afford the hard stuff at all. Just make sure you get something that tastes pleasant, and goes well with your meal.

I know that sounds like heresy, but there has been altogether too much fuss made about wines in the past, and it has tended to make the young hostess terribly timid about introducing them to her own table. The point with wines is, as with everything else in the kitchen department—does it taste good? If you think about it a bit you'll realize without any help that a heavy, dark wine such as port or sweet Madeira won't be the thing to serve with a light, subtle dish such as Rex Sole Meunière—and a gay, giggly wine like champagne isn't quite right with beef-and-kidney pie. Beyond what your instincts tell you, it's silly to get in a fret about the proprieties of wine service. Sophisticated people everywhere tend to form their own patterns in the matter, anyway. My friend the elderly baroness insists upon drinking her sherry over ice, with a twist of Rhangpor lime. Do what you like, and do it with dash and conviction. If it's different, everybody will probably think you are terribly chic.

Another thing you shouldn't worry about is "what year?" for wines. This is a holdover from the past, when grape-growing and winery techniques were far less reliable than they are today. With imported wines, of course, it still does make a difference, here and there. But in California every year is a good year—so buy California wines, and save yourself a lot of money and worry. I am told by the most reliable source I know on this subject, a great connoisseur of wines who lives in Boston and goes to the continent every year to stock up on supplies for his private "cellar," that only a very few, quite extraordinary French wines can beat the wines of California—and that the Frenchman's "vin ordinaire" is far less good than ours, as a general rule.

As for hard liquor, here is a little commentary I wrote a number of years ago:

> A person who is trying to live a Christian life is thrown from the way, because of some close friend who influenced him to drink. Drink not only makes a person senseless and irresponsible, it harms the body and hastens death. Waurika has seven bars and they all do a thriving business. It is really dangerous to walk down the Main Street on a Saturday night because of all of the drunk people.

My mother carefully preserved this little gem of mine, and sent it on, for my amusement, when I "arrived" as a hostess in the wicked city of San Francisco. By this time I had learned that social drinking isn't sinful, and that, providing it's never used as a crutch, it can cause a good deal of innocent merriment. Like most hostesses I was already quite thoroughly involved in the ancient and honorable controversy about which is the right way to mix a dry martini.

Here's the Montandon formula, based on several years' experience in The City That Knows How. Mix it four-to-one, gin or vodka to vermouth, and stir over ice (never shake) until chilled. Pour at once into thoroughly chilled glasses, and serve with a twist of lemon rind, a green olive or a cocktail onion. Many people like their martinis over ice ("on the rocks") in an old-fashioned glass these days, and a "Gibson" is simply a martini served this way, with a cocktail onion rather than olive or lemon peel.

In the small household, and this includes us working girls, it's hospitable to have a sideboard or bar table in your living room, where guests can mix their own drinks. Have ice in an insulated bucket, mixes and olives, onions, limes and lemons or other garnishes on hand.

In other parts of the country people have different drinking habits, so find out what is expected, in the way of supplies, in your own community. San Franciscans tend to ask most often for Scotch and vodka. At a cocktail party for fifty people in San Francisco, you can expect that guests will consume five bottles of Scotch to one and a half bourbon and two of vodka or gin. At a dinner party the amount consumed will be much less, of course, because you will end the cocktail hour after two or three rounds of drinks. But in any case you should always buy more than you think you need, and then return the bottles, unopened, after the party to your dealer if you wish. You should keep a supply of apéritifs on hand: sherry, Dubonnet and vermouth, and on your bar table you'll want a supply of ice water, tonic and mixers such as ginger ale and soda. If you're having a dinner party, you will serve an appropriate wine with dinner, and then offer champagne and/or cognac after dinner if you can afford it.

Don't bother learning to make fancy mixed drinks unless, of course, there is some special favorite in your community at the moment. If you can mix a good martini you're doing fine—and if you can get some attractive man to do it for you you're doing even better! Manhattans and

122

old-fashioneds are Out; vodka "neat" or Scotch-on-the-rocks is In.

MEN.

The field is wide open to the single girl who entertains beautifully. Your real problem will be an embarrassment of riches, as far as men are concerned. You can afford to look them over carefully: the bachelors in your office—the single men you meet at other parties—the boys from back home—the men you meet at resorts, on the tennis court, at the beach—the men you work with on committees or in clubs—the friends-of-friends who are sent to look you up, the visitors you entertain from other parts of the country and other parts of the world. If you give good parties, 99 out of 100 of these characters would adore to come and drink your liquor and eat your food for you—so be a bit hardheaded about just which ones you decide to include on your party lists. It's one thing to run a soup kitchen, and another to mix a guest list that's heady and stimulating. It isn't necessary to mix men to women four to one at your parties, but I think the men you do invite are about four times as important as the women in setting the tone and the pace of your party. So ask yourself—who the men are in your party life at the moment, and what they are doing there. Answer this question frankly, and you may be in for some surprises—or some basic reorganization which will be good for everyone concerned.

MEN YOU *DO* WANT FOR PARTIES

1. Your Party Buddy. First of all, of course, there is your Party Buddy, or Buddies. A clever girl who knows her own mind can have a number of male friends who *are* friends. She doesn't mess with their deeper emotions, and they don't mess with hers. It's true comradeship, on the lighter side, and the relationship is valuable to everyone involved. It's especially helpful to the single girl to have the aid and protection of at least one male friend when she is entertaining large groups. So when you look at men, look for brothers as well as lovers, and if you find comfortable relationships of this sort, by all means be content to keep it this way. Men are tired of being pursued by aggressive women these days, and you needn't apologize for not offering to jump into bed with a man you happen to like. He'll probably be grateful to find a buddy for a change —a girl who's perfectly happy with a sisterly role in his life. You'll have fun together, and it will all be very relaxed.

2. *The Big Man in Your Life.* We'll assume that you're in love—or that you'd like to be. The woman who isn't and doesn't want to be is only half alive! You'll want to invite *the* man to your party, and in fact you may have invented the entire occasion purely for his benefit— whether he knows it or not. One of your best ploys in the love game is a superb party with yourself as hostess. There you are, drifting around by candlelight, looking marvelous in your little chiffon whatsis—*and you can even cook, too!* You've arranged everything beautifully, you've filled your home with charming friends—and, because you've used all the helpful little hints in this book, it seems completely effortless. There's no better way for a girl to show off. At her own party she is Venus and Goddess of the Hearth, all in one. So by all means invite that man, and show him what you can do!

3. *The Amiable Neuter.* You know the kind of man I mean? He doesn't chase you (or anybody else, presuma-

bly) around the bed after hours, but he's absolutely great at parties. Sometimes he's the one who knows how to play the piano, or he's a fabulous conversationalist. He's the one you count on, to amuse the guest of honor, to flatter your female guests, to converse easily with males of any sort, and to rescue potential wallflowers before they have become rooted in their corners. He knows everybody, it seems, and can talk knowledgably about any subject that's mentioned. Chameleonlike, he absorbs the mood of any party he goes to. He accepts people the way they are, doesn't demand or offer too much or too little, comes to the party on time, in a cheerful frame of mind, stays cheerful for as many hours as the party lasts—and when 2 A.M. arrives is sincerely delighted to drive your great-uncle to the airport, because it just happens he was going that way himself. Blessings on The Amiable Neuter! He is every hostess' dream, and he should be on every party list in the nation, as a permanent fixture!

4. *The Interesting Misfit.* By this I don't mean the man who comes to the party with socks that don't match, or the man who stands behind the kitchen door all evening biting his fingernails—I mean the person who adds interest to your group because he is a little different—in age, in type, in status, in talent or ability, in background or experience. A party made up entirely of middle-class suburbanites between the ages of thirty and thirty-five, for example, is bound to be a bore. The clever hostess adds to this group at least one person who is quite different—a traveler from abroad, a sprinkling of artists from the city, an elderly widower who is a raconteur of great charm and ability, or a subgroup, perhaps, of younger men, still involved in the college scene or excited about the hippie movement. Parties are *alive* when they provide a meeting ground for

people with different interests, and you yourself will be more alive if you include men of all ages and types, in your party world. Just make sure you don't invite too many men who will loathe each other upon first meeting, or you will have fistfights in the foyer—and remember that a party made up of nothing *but* Interesting Misfits is not going to be very interesting either. What you want is a deft balance of comfort and spice—for yourself, for the other women present, and for the group as a whole.

5. *The Good Fairy.* As party guests many of these gentlemen are interesting, attractive, amusing, and very well-behaved. They'll enjoy talking with your female guests about art and travel, fashion, décor and clothes— any subject dear to the feminine heart—and their manners will be courtly and gallant, if they are the type I have in mind. Men of this sort should be added to your guest list with caution, though, as you'd add curry or garlic to the entree, by the quarter-teaspoonful, not by the ladleful. They're spicy and fun, but you don't want to overwhelm your other guests with the flavor they bring to the group. And remember, too, there are some square-cut male types, rather musclebound in the brains department, who positively froth at the mouth at any hint of male homosexuality, so don't try to mix these two types at a small gathering or you're in for trouble.

Mr. AC-DC is the trickiest type of all to deal with socially. He's crazy about women, bless his heart—but he just adores men too. If he's witty and well-mannered he can be a great delight as a party guest. But beware—and this is one of the times when you'd be wise to do a little discreet research into his party habits. Call a mutual friend, if you're in doubt, and ask. If you introduce him to an attractive young couple will he instantly try to seduce the wife—or the husband—or both? Does he swing from the chandeliers, after the third drink—and if so, alone or in company? If you plan to invite the riot squad to your party in any case, Mr. AC-DC should definitely be on your list.

MEN YOU DON'T WANT AT PARTIES

Obviously, the number one man you don't want at your party is the one you didn't invite:

1. The Crasher. The more successful you are as a hostess the more you'll have to worry about crashers, unfortunately. Since my own parties have become famous this has become a major problem for me, and it is necessary for me to have a maid or a friend stationed at the door to check a guest list. If two people with the same name show up it's time for a look-see. This can and does happen, because the Crasher merely mentions a name he has seen frequently on the society pages. Your helper must be tactful, at moments like this, or you had better handle it yourself.

What do you say to a Crasher, once you've spotted him? I'm convinced that it doesn't matter much, really, what you say. Anyone brazen enough to crash a party isn't apt to have very delicate sensibilities when he's caught at it; and the point is to remove him from the scene without disturbing the other guests.

At my Mod Party, one man arrived nattily dressed for the occasion in hip-hugging pants, a striped shirt and cap —and a face I had never seen before. I walked over to him and said, "I don't think we've met."

"No, we haven't," he replied. "Who are you?"

"I'm your hostess, Pat Montandon." He wasn't in the least embarrassed. "Hi," he replied. "Have a drink?"

"Are you here with someone?" I asked him.

"Oh sure," he said, but he wasn't able to be specific, so I suggested mildly that he depart.

"Well," he snapped, "I don't think you're very hospitable!"

That did it! I took the drink out of his hand and said, "No, I'm not. And if I were as hospitable as you'd like me to be, the whole city of San Francisco would be here." This crasher left quietly when he saw that I meant business, but it is always best to have a friend on call in case of any unpleasantness. Crashers can be amazingly rude and shameless at times.

2. *Drunks and Other Sorrows.* Drinking is fun, but drunkenness isn't—for the hostess and the other guests. Most of us know people in our circle of friends who have full-fledged drinking problems, and we watch out for them. It's kinder, as well as more sensible, not to invite them to a free-swinging cocktail party; better entertain them quietly some other time, and serve coffee or tea. The occasional social drunk is another sort of problem—the individual who under certain circumstances of tension or fatigue isn't able to drink well but insists upon drinking far too much anyway. Keep your eyes open at your parties for situations like this, and whisper a word to your bartender *before* your guest gets glassy-eyed. He can water down the drinks or make excuses for not serving the potential troublemaker too often.

The most dangerous drunk of all at a party is the uptight, "cool" drunk who looks as sober as a portrait of somebody's Presbyterian ancestor but is actually whacked right out of his mind. You never can tell what one of these types is going to do when he finally goes over the brink. I saw one frightfully dignified gentleman of this sort march very deliberately into the glass front of an heirloom

128

grandfather clock, and when it toppled over onto him, completely smashed to bits, he lay on the floor happily intoning excerpts from the "Song of Solomon" until he was escorted to the coatroom by the butler. One of the other guests remarked, "Why can't he wear a wristwatch like everybody else?" but it really wasn't funny, because the hostess loved that clock, and it was absolutely irreplaceable.

A drunken guest is often a wildly amorous one as well. A little by-play at parties is all to the good, but if your female guests are being pinched black and blue and husbands are beginning to challenge the offender to public duel, it's time for you to remove him or have him removed. Don't be impressed by the overtures of a drunken guest yourself, either! Alcohol, contrary to general opinion, is no love potion. True, it may give a man ideas, but it doesn't help him to carry them out. The drunk who pursues you around the coffee table late in the evening would probably be just as happy out in the foyer necking with somebody's mink coat. So let him do that while you call a taxi to take him home. He's in no condition to drive—so he's certainly in no condition to make love to you.

3. Big Daddy. The much-older-man who cruises the party scene in your community may be a perfectly nice guy, just lonesome, and looking around for some tender little morsel to keep him satisfied in his declining years. On the other hand he may be plenty of trouble. Unless you know him very well indeed, and are quite sure he's not one of the "dirty old man" variety, you don't want one of these as your Party Buddy, and you certainly don't want to become indebted to him in any way. A girl I know once made the mistake of accepting a great deal of help, comfort and protection—as well as several diamond brooches and a very pretty emerald bracelet, from an elderly man who treated her just like his favorite daughter —until one night when she had to call the vice squad to rescue her. My friend was a sadder and much wiser young lady after this experience. "Pat," she told me, "I don't know what the older generation is coming to—but I'm going to play with kids my own age from now on."

If you are married and Big Daddy happens to be your husband's boss, you may have a special problem with him. Some of these men come on strong, and actually imply that the husband's career may be at stake if the wife won't play Party Games and any other kind of games he has in mind. Avoid being alone with a man like this, and if he tries to corner you excuse yourself quickly to attend to some hostess duty. Be cordial and courteous, but absolutely cool, with him. Let him tell everyone in town you're frigid, if necessary—but don't do *anything* to encourage him or you'll be sorry. Many of these men are just playing around, and don't seriously believe that they have their employees' wives in their power. But if it's really bad, tell your husband about it, *after the party*. Always do everything possible to avoid any kind of a scene when guests are present. Nothing can ruin a party quicker than harsh words or quarreling.

4. *Pillar of the Community* (Dr. Jekyll-Mr. Hyde). You've met a really Big Wheel—president of the biggest corporation in the city—political boss—movie star—journalist who's the toast of the town—someone everyone you know would love to meet. The very thought of inviting him to your next party gives you the happy collywobbles. But be sure that you want to have this man to your party, with your friends, at your home. What do you really know about him, anyway? He thought *you* were pretty

cute, the other evening when he met you. Then have lunch with him a few times and look him over objectively, not as a reputation, but as a man. Several up-and-coming girls I know have neglected to do this, and could tell you stories about the results that would make you have the *other* kind of collywobbles.

I made this mistake myself once several years ago, and although I know it sounds dramatic, it almost cost me the life of one of my dearest friends. I invited a very distinguished man to one of my dinner parties—a civic leader with a sound and conservative reputation in business circles—a true "pillar of the community" whom I knew in a personal way hardly at all. We had met only briefly, but I had found him quite impressive in his office, discussing business matters in a learned tone.

He came to the party, held forth brilliantly for the first few hours or so on various matters of general interest, and then, over a very dark highball (which he had mixed for himself—and I suddenly realized that he had mixed quite a few for himself, just as strong as this one) he sank into a moody silence and began staring in an odd, angry way at my friend Margot across the room. Soon he and Margot were deep in private conversation, and I thought no more of it until they left together. He had offered to drive her home.

The next morning Margot telephoned me with her teeth chattering. "I've never been so frightened in my life," she said. "He's completely insane. I didn't think I'd get home alive! The minute we got into the car he began to scream and curse at me, and he headed out on the freeway going north at eighty miles an hour."

He had announced to Margot that they were going up to his fishing lodge on the coast, and hole up there until the end of the world (which he said was due the following week). He had plenty of guns, he said, and he would show her what a good shot he was as soon as they arrived. Luckily, Margot had the presence of mind to agree heartily with this plan, and asked him only to drive her to her apartment first, so she could get some more suitable clothes. After a wild ride back into the city, and up and down the rain-slick hills of San Francisco, she finally got him to stop in front of her apartment. He followed her in, she ran out again, and he locked himself in her apartment and began wrecking everything in sight. Margot called the police from the phone booth on the corner, and when they arrived, Mr. Prominent Citizen was sitting peaceably in front of Margot's TV set in his crumpled dinner jacket, watching the Late-Late Show. He was highly insulted at being invited to leave before he could see how the story came out, and he gave the policemen quite a self-righteous little lecture about how they ought to be attending to their civic duties among the beatniks in the slums, and not bothering distinguished citizens at the higher levels of Society.

The police were unimpressed and escorted him firmly home, but Margot was badly shaken up by the experience. I've never forgiven myself for allowing it to happen. In a sense of course the responsibility was hers—after all she is a grown person, and she agreed to go home with this man. But as a hostess I was to blame. When you invite people to your home you are giving them your personal seal of approval. You are recommending them to your other friends. So be careful whom you recommend.

5. *Honey Bun.* Two hundred and one pounds of fun, that was Nelson—six feet three, with a glowing Malibu Beach tan, and muscles rippling divinely under his sexy

collection of polo shirts and silk dinner jackets. He was the life of the party everywhere he went, and for a number of months he flew in regularly from the Southland and made quite a thing of chasing me around town—in public, that is. In private it was a different matter, and I began to wonder whether I was losing my sex appeal. Nelson always said goodnight, with some little joke or other, at the front door of my apartment, and when he finally got around to kissing me goodnight I found that this very definitely didn't turn *me* on, either. Oh well, I thought, I guess the old chemistry just isn't there between us. So I decided to give a dinner party, and introduce him to a very nice girl I knew, who had recently been divorced.

Dorothy arrived at the party looking absolutely smashing in a very low-cut black Dior number, and beamed in on Nelson, as per instructions, from the start. His reaction— or so it seemed—was terrific. He was funnier than ever, and held everyone spellbound with his jokes and capers, which grew wilder and wilder as the evening progressed. Finally it began to dawn on me—and on the other guests as well, I'm sure—that the occasion for all this excitement was not Dorothy at all. Poor me! Poor Dorothy! The person Nelson was flirting with all this time was a friend of ours I'll call George.

Now George is a talented musician, with great personal charms, and he is also a homosexual—a fact which he does not try to conceal. But on the other hand he doesn't make a public nuisance of himself about it, either. When Nelson started trying to demonstrate judo holds on poor old George amid my very best brandy glasses and demitasse cups after dinner, George developed a sudden "headache" and courteously departed. Nelson was inconsolable, of course, and the party broke up, very awkwardly, long before midnight. I felt like a terrible failure as hostess and friend and was really quite furious.

But this was not the end of the trouble caused by this particular Honey Bun. The next day George telephoned me, laughing, and told me, "Pat, I never thought I'd be competition for you or Dorothy, but that Nelson friend of yours has been calling me since seven o'clock this morning begging for a date."

I was appalled and fascinated. "What are you going to do about it?" I asked.

"I haven't decided yet," George replied. "You know that headache I mentioned last night—well, I really *have* it, now."

A week later he telephoned me again. "Look," he said, "next time Nelson's in town, tell him I've gone to Mexico or something, will you?"

"What happened?" I asked him.

"Well, I made the most beautiful picnic for Honey Bun you ever saw in your life," George replied mournfully. "A thermos of iced vichysoisse, salmon in aspic, cucumbers in sour cream, and chilled papaya with mint leaves . . . Sauvignon Blanc, two bottles . . . the works."

"Yes . . ."

"We drove out to the country and found a nice haystack on a farm. While I set up the supper *your* friend Nelson went into his *routine,* roaring up and down the haystack shouting at the top of his lungs like a complete idiot, and of course the farmer heard him and came out to see what was going on. He took one look at the two of us and all our gear and he threatened to call the sheriff, but fast. Nelson was still giggling and hopping around like a maniac. I've never been so furious in my life."

They went in search of another idyllic spot, but this

time they landed directly under a wasp's nest, and had to move on again after packing and unpacking everything once more. Nelson was still joking around, and George was in a rage. Back to the city they drove, and ate their mangled meal in George's apartment. Whereupon Nelson cracked a few more jokes, kissed his host goodnight, and disappeared, still chortling!

"Let's *all* forget about Nelson *permanently*," said George. And I wish I could say that we did, but unfortunately he cropped up in my life one more time when I was having dinner with some friends at a restaurant in San Francisco. Radiant as always with his Southern California tan, muscles bulging under the dinner jacket, he strode across the room. He made a great noise about greeting me, and gave everyone to understand that we were very dear old friends indeed. Perhaps there was something of enthusiasm lacking in my own greeting, for after a few moments' conversation his eyes narrowed as he looked at me and he turned away from our table—remarking loudly to my companions as he left, "You know, Pat has the *hardest* bed in town."

Nice guy, Nelson! Remember him when you make up your next party list, and for your own good be sure to include him out.

CHAPTER EIGHT

Pipers Must Be Paid

"How about 10,000 crickets doing a precision drill under the coffee table?"

"Or maybe 307 albino canaries singing an aria sotto voce?"

My friend Wally Wood and I were brainstorming far-out ideas for a charity party I'd been asked to produce. Precision-drilled crickets and albino canaries were part of the loosening-up process we always use to free our imaginations while we try to think of something new and exciting. It's great to have a partner at this point in your thinking about a party, so you can bounce the ideas back and forth, and I count myself very lucky indeed to have Wally's help. He is a marvelously talented young man and will be well-known as a first-rate artist someday.

After a bit of experience in party-giving you will undoubtedly develop a sort of Talent Trust of people you call in to advise you on party ideas and all the problems of carrying them out. Some are volunteers, others must be paid; but in any case they usually give far more of their time and talent than you've dared hope, if they get carried away with the party idea.

137

If money is no object you can, in most cities, turn to a catering service which will take your idea and follow it through in every detail. The Party Givers, for example, in San Francisco are prepared to put on a routine party for a client or to stage a highly elaborate one following a theme of the client's choice. Recently the mother of a debutante here wanted to give a circus party for her daughter, and she turned the problem over to the Party Givers. They produced a three-ring extravaganza which would have been impossible without professional help.

The party was given in the country, starting with swimming at 4 P.M.While the young people played in and out of the pool, the caterer's staff of twenty-three, all in circus costumes, were in constant attendance. There were barkers for games of chance, an organ grinder and his monkey, an electric calliope and a ringmaster with a megaphone, who directed the young guests and announced the circus acts. After swimming the guests watched acrobats, a professional karate demonstration, seven chimpanzees who played rock-'n-roll music with instruments and a fire-eater whose finale consisted of jumping through a circle of blazing daggers.

This was probably more of a circus than any of the younger generation had ever seen before. The catering service provided popcorn in red and white paper bags, and machines to spin sugar and snow cones. Later there was a seated dinner with waiters in circus outfits, and the Party Givers also brought a band for dancing after dinner.

For one hundred guests it cost in the neighborhood of $10,000, which isn't bad, considering that some deb parties run to $25,000 and more. In a season of very elaborate parties this was the one the young people appreciated most, and I believe it is worth noting that the party was remarkable for another reason—the hostess did not serve liquor to her young guests. Liquor is considered a "must" at the deb parties here, even though many of the young people do not know how to handle it at seventeen and eighteen, and I have great admiration for the hostess who dared to be different.

The Party Givers and similar firms can do practically anything you want in the way of unusual entertaining. In smaller towns and cities it isn't as easy to get professional help, but you can probably find talent among florists, the display staffs of local department stores or the production department of the local theatre. When you ask for assistance don't pretend you know everything! Be frank to admit you can't drive a nail straight, paint a backdrop or arrange flowers. Once the people with these skills get interested in your party idea there will be no stopping them —and you, meanwhile, can watch and learn.

Suppose that you wanted to give a circus party in a location where no one like the Party Givers was available, and that your budget was nothing at all like $10,000. I would suggest that you proceed by calling the local high school first of all, and try to interest the kids there in your project. Maybe they have a marching band with drum majorettes who would like a chance to perform. Generally there's a "character" on campus who would love to be a clown for a party like this. Maybe there's a barbershop quartet, and a group that could put on skits with your help and the cooperation of the drama department. You could decorate your yard inexpensively with huge swags of crêpe paper, and scout your town for balloons and other decorations. Maybe there's an organ-grinder man with his monkey who'd like to be part of the festivities.

"Paint with a broad brush," says Wally Wood. "The

most important thing in the end is your guests. They love to be amused by interesting décor, but décor isn't everything. Give them something fun to *do*."

Wally likes to keep the surprises coming during a party. "Avoid springing everything at once," he advises. "Try for a delayed reaction by having another room decorated, in addition to the usual ones. An upstairs room with an extra bar, or a special orchestra, is good. Or a study or library where guests unexpectedly find another sort of atmosphere."

If you plan your effects carefully you can keep the costs of all this surprisingly low. Count on all your friends and acquaintances and all the resources of your particular community to help you. You need more than artistic friends and handymen. You need friends who are gourmets and idea people; you need the help of your dressmaker and your hairdresser, to help you get ready for the party. You need those special friends who will come early and help you get through the difficult stage at the start of the party—when many a hostess wonders if it wasn't all a big mistake. You need the teen-aged sons and daughters of your neighbors, and on this I would like to say a few extra words, because I think the teen-agers are *the* great untapped source of talent in our whole society.

It's very hard for teen-agers to get jobs and many of them, I know, feel unwanted and unappreciated by the people around them. This is a terrible mistake, and I am sure it is one of the causes of juvenile delinquency. I have learned from personal experience that these kids are full of wonderful ideas, and willing to work hard to help carry out a good party plan. So by all means give them a chance, and depend on them! They won't let you down. Hire the boys in your neighborhood to park your guests' cars for them, to help you with the heavy work of setting up a party, and ask their advice on music and entertainment too. Give the girls a chance to help with the décor, to sew and cook and wash dishes for you—and let them dress up and be party hostesses with you, serving hors d'oeuvres and checking guest lists, and the like. This sort of semiprofessional help is invaluable, and the good will it creates in the community is worth considering. To the hostess who works with a limited budget the teen-agers in her community can be a Talent Trust that is truly beyond price.

There are parties for all purses, so don't ignore your possibilities as a hostess simply because you think you can't afford the role. It could be more rewarding to you, purely in terms of happiness, than the new suit you buy on a monthly budget plan or the vacation you save for so methodically. Try to have a party budget too, so the money you accumulate will be available on short notice when an important visitor comes to town and you want to entertain. Be prepared to invite friends on a spur-of-themoment basis.

It takes hard work and plenty of realistic thinking to plan a party that doesn't run over your particular budget. Sit down with your pencil and paper the minute you decide to give a party and face facts. Whatever you do, don't hire anyone or buy anything on impulse. Find out exactly what it is going to cost you, well ahead of time, and adjust your sights accordingly. My friend Lucille Sullivan, who manages the showroom of a very handsome contemporary furniture store in San Francisco, is a great expert in party-planning from the budget point of view. Because she has the knack of giving really elegant parties "on a shoestring" her boss has turned over to her the job of giving opening-night parties for the art exhibitions he likes to have in his showroom, and she often manages his private parties as well, when important clients are in town visiting. I have asked Lucille's advice many times myself, and I am happy to share the benefit of her experience here.

"I never sacrifice quality," says Lucille, "but I insist upon getting the most for my money—or for the boss' money! I shop around for the best deal in liquors first, and with me this means getting on a bus and looking around town for bargains. I haven't a car, and I have learned to do a lot of things by phone too, for this reason. For example, I call the major caterers and ask them to send me their expense sheets. I can tell you the exact costs of the ten top caterers in town. I look very carefully at their hors d'oeuvres suggestions, because hors d'oeuvres are apt to be unnecessarily costly. I'm always looking for ways to serve nice food for less money."

For cocktail parties Lucille prefers a bartender to a cateress who handles only the hors d'oeuvres. "Your party is much more elegant if the guests are served by a white-jacketed bartender," she says. "In San Francisco, a bartender hired through a catering service costs $25. Hired on an individual basis, his fee is $15 to $20. So I telephone the employment office of one of the San Francisco colleges, and hire a young man who will work for $10 or less. I rent the white jacket and give him instructions before the party. If he does well I give him a tip or $2 or $4 and keep his name on my list of helpers."

Lucille's other tips include the following: Count the bottles before the party starts and count them with the bartender when it's over. When you are making arrangements for liquor be sure that you can return the unopened bottles. And, as for hors d'oeuvres, don't try to serve anything hot without a cateress, and avoid drippy or greasy foods unless you want to pay expensive cleaning bills for carpets and upholstery.

Lucille keeps a folder on each of her parties, whether it's her own, her boss's or one she was asked to give as a business venture.

"I gave two within a week of each other, one for the opening of an exhibition at the office and the other for the opening of an art gallery. They were exactly alike, except that I was paid a small fee for the gallery party."

Both parties were remarkably reasonable in price. Lucille offered the guests four or five kinds of imported cheese, ripe green apples polished to a shine, green seedless grapes, and assorted kinds of crackers. Champagne too, of course. "I think champagne is elegant for gallery parties, and entirely suitable. But I don't think, in a hard-liquor town, you can get away with *just* champagne at anything but an arty gathering."

Here's how the expenses for the gallery party broke down:

240 invitations	$45
Postage	$12.50
Fruit	$10
Cheese	$20
Crackers	$ 2
Napkins	$ 2
Glasses (incl. ice & tubs)	$15.50
Champagne (3 cases, domestic)	$93.75
Bartender	$15
	$215.75

"We expected about seventy-five people, the average

turnout for this sort of opening, but nearly twice that many turned up," says Lucille. "We had plenty of everything except glasses. I had to keep washing them to help the bartender. The guests loved the food, and it looked very attractive, I must say. I collected cheese boards from my friends, and put the different cheeses on them. The crackers were in one huge tray, and the chilled apples and grapes were lovely together in huge glass bowls. It looked *very* opulent!"

Lucille has ideas on inexpensive flower arrangements too. She shops by bus for flowers for her boss's parties and arranges them at home. "Never cut costs where it shows," she says. She buys masses of daisies, which are inexpensive and good-looking, and makes striking arrangements for two or three dollars for which a florist would be likely to charge five times as much. When the arrangements are complete her boss sends his car for her or pays a taxi to transport his party manager and her flowers to the show-room.

As for party clothes, Lucille generally designs her own and has them made by a dressmaker. She makes all of her own at-home clothes and hostess gowns from interesting drapery fabrics and other unusual materials she picks up at bargain prices. A perfectionist about her apartment, she is decorating it slowly, with the same elegant taste and frugal management she applies to her party-giving career.

Recently Lucille gave an impressive cocktail party for sixty-five friends. She feels the same way I do about sending people out on the road after hours of drinking without giving them something substantial in the way of food. By clever planning Lucille managed to feed her guests an attractive and delicious buffet for about 50 cents per person! She went to a delicatessen where she got a deal on some packaged dinners of superior quality, including sliced beef, ham and turkey, potato salad, rolls and relishes. Twenty of these picnics were unpackaged and arranged attractively on platters for the late-stayers at the party. Previous to this, a caterer provided plenty of little sandwiches as hors d'oeuvres, and Lucille herself had prepared dozens of deviled hardboiled eggs, with curry, so everyone had plenty to eat.

Recently I gave a cocktail party for the same number of people which was a good deal more elaborate than Lucille's, thus more expensive. For purposes of comparison, then, let's look at the plan for my party, which is still here in my notebook with every detail priced and analyzed.

This is a party I gave for my upstairs neighbors, Dania and Bruce Bomberger, whose apartment I have borrowed for so many parties. I decided it was time I gave something a bit lavish for them, and since they are both artists the theme that naturally developed was that of a gallery party, with their paintings on display upstairs and down.

We started to talk about the party three months ahead of time, and the date was set. Because it was to be rather large we checked the date with society editors; and in order to suggest that it was a formal occasion I had invitations engraved. The invitations were sent out a month in advance of the party.

We called in Wally Wood, and the four of us had a brainstorming session. The main thing to consider, we decided, was the art—how the paintings should be hung and lighted to best advantage, and how we could make sure that guests saw all of them. We planned to take all the furniture out of the back bedroom again and decided to staple the walls with plain white no-seam papers as a gallery background. The buffet table would be in this room to lure the guests in.

Bruce had done five very fine portraits of prominent

San Franciscans, and we decided to put these in a conspicuous place in the living room, above my big white sofa. All the paintings were to have special lighting—overhead for the portraits, spots for the others. Groupings of paintings would be hung in the hallways and up the stairs, and in the Bombergers' apartment above another display would be on view.

Party helpers were hired as soon as the day was set. We decided upon three maids and a bartender, and after reserving the date with them I arranged to have a special conference with the chief maid, who would arrive early in the afternoon to get the food ready. We wanted to serve something substantial, and after some discussion we settled upon a large New York strip, baked and sliced, to go with sourdough French bread slices, and small chicken drumsticks, fried and dressed with frills, since they were to be eaten in the fingers—plus stuffed pullet eggs, and various cheeses with rye bread and crackers. This was solid fare, nothing too exotic or distracting.

Next in my notes I find that I called a rental agency and ordered highball glasses (twice as many as the number of guests), a dozen ashtrays, a rack for coats, and a tub for ice. I arranged for the bartender to bring the ice when he arrived at 5 P.M. the day of the party (one hour before the party was due to start) and I ordered the liquor—Scotch, bourbon, gin, vodka, mixes, soft drinks, tomato juice, limes and lemons.

And now a wonderful bit of luck came my way. I had wanted to have music at the party—I generally do—and yet it's always a difficult item in the budget. While we were still in the planning stage of things I stopped in one evening at a San Francisco night spot called The Library, and heard a wonderful folk-rock combo called the Samuel

146

Peeps. I asked them if they were free the evening of my party, and said if they were I wanted to talk about having them play.

The next day their leader called and said they had heard so much about my parties they would be delighted to play without charge. The cocktail hour is not a busy period for them, he explained, and they would be glad to have the exposure to a different group of people from the ones who usually came to The Library. It was an ideal arrangement all around.

The night before the party, I remember, was pretty wild—it usually is. I always fix a casserole ahead of time, so my helpers and I can eat whenever we are hungry. The house is cleaned thoroughly during the day, and in the evening we really settle down to work. The rented things were delivered, and we straightened them out. Wally arrived to help hang the paintings, while the rest of us ran around setting up the party scene. One small hitch—Wally cut the wrong wire fixing a spotlight, and the lights went out all over the apartment! No one could find the right fuse box, so there was nothing to do but wait for the repairmen. We passed the time pleasantly enough, with a little supper by candlelight.

I made a diagram of the buffet table for the maids, so they would know where to put each of the trays and platters, the candelabra and the centerpiece. The menu was pasted up in the kitchen (it's terrible to open the refrigerator the next day and find a bowl of crab legs or some other delicacy that was never brought to your guests!) We arranged flowers—big, handsome bouquets of chrysanthemums and dahlias—and built the makings of a small fire in the fireplace—nothing to drive a guest away with its heat, just enough to be cheerful.

By 1 A.M. every painting was hung, each spot was in place, the items on my list were all crossed off, and all we had to do was get a night's sleep and get ourselves ready for the party. The next day more flowers arrived, needing to be arranged, and I had a few last-minute duties to attend to (such as putting cigarettes around, and final checking), but in the main we were ready. I could concentrate on my own clothes for the party, my hairdo and personal appearance. It's worth staying up late the night before to be this far ahead of the game.

And here are the expenses for our very successful Gallery Party:

Meat, chicken and shrimp	$67
Bread and cheese	$ 5
Other food, miscellaneous	$17
Flowers	$15
Rental (glasses, coatrack, ashtrays)	$17.50
Frills for drumsticks	$ 2.75
Invitations	$16
Liquor	$75
Music – free!	
Helpers	$100
	$315.25

Not bad, considering the luxurious atmosphere and service! Several more modest parties could be given for this price, of course, and the party would have been much less expensive had I been willing to sacrifice my idea of serving substantial food and having plenty of waitresses. But everything turned out just the way I wanted it, so I had nothing to complain about.

One excellent way of cutting costs in half or even in quarters is to give the party with other people. If you want a fairly lavish setup be sure to consider this as a possibility. Two young hostesses I know have worked together on parties quite often, pooling their talents (one is a marvelous cook, the other a professional decorator) and sharing their equipment, so there is no rental cost for glasses, dishes and so forth. With two hostesses on hand you need less in the way of hired help, and all the responsibilities of party-giving, including the financial responsibility, become much simpler to manage. Just make sure each of you knows *exactly* what she is expected to do, and make out a schedule with carbon copy, so you won't be disappointed in each other at the last moment!

One of the best cocktail-buffet parties I have ever been to was given by two women working together in this way. One owned a lovely house with a sunken living room, where the party took place. The mood of the evening was Samoan, for one of the hostesses, a journalist, had written an article about a troupe of Samoan entertainers, and they gratefully volunteered to perform when they heard about the party. The warmth of these charming people turned the evening into a festival of South Seas song and dance. It was a fairly large and lavish party, with bartender, plenty of liquor and a hearty buffet. The total cost was $95, which would put a crimp in most budgets, but divided in half it was very reasonable.

If you would pay $18.15 for a new hat then you can give a party for that price instead. Here's how four young working girls gave an elegant party for $18.15 each, with twenty-four guests, a maid, liquor, flowers and a lovely dinner. A friend of theirs was leaving town to take an exciting new job in New York, so the girls got together and decorated one of their apartments with posters and pictures of the big city. (Cost—nothing. One of them worked at a travel agency.) They invited their favorite men to take over the bartending duties, and shopped carefully for the best buys in liquor. They prepared all the food ahead of time, and kept the menu simple: spaghetti, green salad, pastries, coffee and wine. All the maid had to do was boil the spaghetti and add their special sauce to it, slice the French bread, and serve.

The girls bought an inexpensive California chablis by the gallon and served it in attractive decanters. After dinner, instead of liqueurs or highballs they continued to serve the wine, and beer. The total cost of this delightful and memorable party was $72.60, which, divided four ways, is not much of a hat at that.

You can entertain for less than this if you're willing to try some offbeat ideas. Get outdoors—and you don't have to decorate. Combine some sports activity with your party—touch football on the beach, tennis in the park, badminton in your back yard—and you don't have to provide entertainment. Plan cleverly, enlist the help of friends, and eliminate the need for hired hands. Cooperate with others in the preparation of food and the purchasing of liquor—and you don't have to break the bank.

One enterprising young couple I know challenged their friends to walk across the Golden Gate Bridge on Sunday morning, hike down the mountainside to Sausalito, and meet for lunch there on the waterfront. Eight accepted the challenge, and a ninth volunteered to bring the picnic lunch over by station wagon, provided he didn't have to walk! It was a lovely sunny day, with whitecaps on the Bay, and we all enjoyed our healthy outing. Lunch was a cooperative venture and amazingly lavish—everyone, it seems, had emptied the larder before leaving home. Because we used what we had at hand to prepare this great feast, it's impossible to say *exactly* how much it cost, but I do know that the cash outlay, for eleven people having a wonderful party that lasted all day, was absolutely not one cent!

CHAPTER NINE

Charity Begins at Parties

The word "charity" would never have been mentioned in Waurika, Oklahoma, among the people I knew as a child. People helped one another because it was the decent thing to do. It wouldn't have been considered "charity" to give your needy neighbor a hand, and you'd know that he was prepared to do the same for you should the occasion ever arise.

It's too bad that life can't be as simple in the big cities and in the world at large. Sheer numbers of people make for complication, and we have a great mixture of traditions in America today. Organization is necessary, therefore, in the doing of ordinary good deeds if they are to be effective on a large scale. Across the nation millions of dedicated women are involved in fund-raising projects, ranging from church bazaars and PTA carnivals to an all-out bash like New York's "April in Paris" ball, with profits in the neighborhood of $250,000. Over and over again parties have proved the most painless and by far the most rewarding way of raising money for charitable purposes. Giving parties for charity is a multimillion-dollar business in this country today.

Like any other party it requires careful forethought, but here you are working on an immense scale. Little notes to yourself won't do; you must break down your list of tasks and hand it over in sections to the appropriate committees. You must develop a party with the kind of appeal which will sell tickets; and public relations, in the case of a charity party, are of the very greatest importance. When you sell tickets to a benefit you are promising the public a performance which will be well worth their money, and to the best of your ability you must keep this promise. Your three keys to success are organization, imagination and publicity.

ORGANIZATION

Organization begins with the selection of a chairman. Think this one over carefully, for it's the most important choice you will make. You may have an honorary chairman, someone with a "name" to give your project prestige—but the working chairman you choose will determine the success or failure of the entire venture in the long run. She must be enthusiastic, well-organized and capable of inspiring others to work. Business ability is important, but this does not mean that you should necessarily seek out a high-powered business executive. Frequently these women are far removed from the world of charity affairs, and they antagonize co-workers by being too demanding. The best chairmen are workers who have come up through the ranks of charity parties. They realize clearly that the committee members are not paid but are volunteers—and that the success of the project depends in large part on how well the chairman gets along with them.

The chairman doesn't sit on a pedestal and give orders —she works! Her first job is to check into the records of previous years—not so much to decide what to do as what *not* to do. A good organization will have complete records of past parties in every detail, and she should learn from these how to save money this year and how to operate more efficiently. Perhaps some jobs can be done by volunteers instead of paid help, or certain expensive equipment can be borrowed this year, instead of rented. Maybe she can swing a big donation to cover one of the major items on the budget. Having checked the records thoroughly, the chairman now closes the books and begins to think ahead. The party must be entirely new this year. Nothing must be repeated—including the mistakes of her predecessors!

The next job of the chairman is to select a steering committee. These are the women who will head up various aspects of the party program such as ticket selling, decorations, food, music, program notes and so forth. They must be carefully chosen for their ability to get along together and with the subcommittees they will head. You ought to consider the circumstances and background before you ask any woman to assume an important job of this sort. Is she tied down with small children? Involved with too many other volunteer activities to do justice to the job? Has she proved her ability on other committees? How does her emotional stability rate? Committee work at times can be tense and exhausting.

It's a good idea to select your committee from various social groups, so that a wide range of people will be interested in your party. In a large metropolitan area you will have chairmen in the various suburbs, if your party is likely to attract this large a group.

For a large party, organization starts a full year in advance. The chairman is selected, the date set, and the committees begin to form. Early meetings are necessary to determine many important details, starting with the theme of your party.

IMAGINATION

Above all, think big! Your private parties can be as modest and casual as you like, but a charity party has got to be a spectacular blast or it's a failure from the beginning. Brainstorming sessions with the idea people in your Talent Trust *can* be the most important part of this whole project. Let yourself go, conjure up the wildest and most improbable ideas you can possibly imagine—then, when you have a list of these, take a long, cool look at the situation and decide which one will really *work*. You have got to be completely practical and realistic, of course, but unless you give yourself a chance to pipe-dream *first* your party is likely to be a thud.

Here are some ideas that have been used successfully in a number of cities across the nation. If you decide to adopt any of them be sure to invent your own variations, and think of angles which will appeal in your own community.

1. House Tours. What kinds of houses are people curious about in your area? Old houses? Country Estates? Elegant new penthouse apartments? Bachelor pads? One tour in San Francisco featured houses which had survived the 1906 disaster; another, at $10 a head, offered six fine country places, with the attendance limited to four hundred. Office and industry tours have raised money very successfully for the Senior Center here, by including such intriguing places as a Chinese Fortune Cookie factory, as well as a number of plush executive suites.

House tours are practically all profit. You arrange for

people to donate their homes. Florists will usually decorate free of charge in exchange for a card of credit. Fashions suitable to the places on display may be donated by local stores for members of your group to model. Your main expense will be refreshments—tea, coffee and/or cocktails, to be provided at a party scene at one of the stops.

2. *Fashion Shows* are sure-fire in some cities. It depends, though, on how fashion-conscious people are in your area and, ultimately, upon how much they are willing to pay to see this sort of show. If you give a fashion show luncheon, and the lunch costs your organization $4 per person, you'll have to charge a good deal more than that for tickets or you won't make any money.

Your fashion show will need a spectacular gimmick or a novel theme of some sort to be really successful, so do plenty of thinking about it. You'll need girls with modeling experience. If you have plenty of attractive members in your organization who are willing to take a few lessons from a professional in the field you are ahead of the game. Professional models are expensive, but if you can afford it a few dazzling dames will add a good deal to the glamour of your show. You'll need music, of course, and a runway—which should be carpeted. The clatter of models' feet can be quite deafening otherwise. Music should not be deafening, either. You want your commentator to be clearly heard, and the violins should be in the background, among the potted plants.

3. *A Queen Contest.* This is a highly efficient (if somewhat cold-blooded) way of making money for a good cause. The San Francisco Mardi Gras, sponsored by the Little Jim Club of Children's Hospital, seldom earns less than $50,000 and once hit $70,000 in a Queen Contest at 10 cents a vote. An adroit committee selects about ten

women and invites them to run for Queen of the Shrove Tuesday party. It's all for charity, of course, but things eventually get to a stage where fathers, husbands, relatives and friends are involved in a frantic race to get their own candidates elected. Checks for as much as $10,000 are written on final voting night.

Each Queen organizes her own campaign, writes letters to friends asking for contributions and has a "manager" who drums up publicity by staging little benefits. Voting night brings a fabulous party for contestants, relatives, friends and interested observers. The medical benefits at Children's Hospital are forgotten as rivalries develop and the candidates are pitted against one another for cold cash.

4. Theatre Parties. Theatre parties are popular, whether they are for the opening of a play or a new film. A charity group can take over the entire house or just a block of tickets, and charge extra prices, with the difference going for good works. It's smart to have a party before or after the performance, too, to earn more money. These are not terribly lucrative benefits, but they do provide valuable publicity for the group.

When Carol Channing came to San Francisco in *Hello Dolly!* a group of Bennington graduates saw a chance for a benefit—Carol had gone to Bennington before making it big as a Broadway star. With an okay from producer David Merrick they planned a package deal, including theatre ticket and supper at Trader Vic's, where Miss Channing agreed to meet everyone after the show. Tickets were sold at $25 apiece, which was a good value, considering that scalpers were getting $15 and $20 for opening-night seats alone. A large block of tickets was sold successfully and a memorable opening night was enjoyed by everyone concerned.

5. *Debutante Balls*. The old snob system isn't what it used to be. Everybody wants to get into the society act these days, and the Charity Debutante Ball is the happy invention which has made it possible, provided Papa has the wherewithal.

In the bad old days in San Francisco there was only one deb ball—the Cotillion—which was strictly for daughters of the prominent local families. Nowadays we have three deb balls in the suburbs and two in San Francisco. All the newcomers are benefits, with the families "donating" up to $1,000 per girl. A good many cities have discovered that the debutante ball is a very enjoyable and efficient way of making money for charity. It's the Affluent Society's answer to the old, old snob system. If the affluent group in your own community has unsatisfied social ambitions, a benefit ball for debutantes will be a sure-fire moneymaker for the cause you have in mind.

6. *Charity Balls* are old favorites, constantly in need of new formats and fresh inspiration. Let your imagination run free on this one! Theme, décor and entertainment should be as lavish and alluring as you can possibly manage. Don't be halfhearted when you plan a charity ball— make up your mind to involve your entire community in the biggest blast anyone has ever seen!

My friend Lila, who moved to San Francisco several years before I did, tells me she'll never forget the first "Black and White Ball" that was ever given in San Francisco. This is a benefit for the San Francisco Symphony, which was such a wild success that it has been repeated, by popular demand, several years in a row. People who were used to the ordinary "benefit" were stunned that first year when they found that a ticket to this dance meant that they would waltz to a full orchestra conducted by Andre Kostelanetz at the Sheraton-Palace Hotel and then go on to three other hotel ballrooms with three different kinds of décor and music during the evening. Shuttle buses carried the celebrants from one place to another, and the entire city was in a state of excitement until daybreak. "I never did find my shoes," Lila tells me, "but it was the best party I've ever been to in my life!"

The "Black and White Ball" has been widely imitated in other cities, in one form or another. It's an all-out effort, involving hundreds of volunteer workers and the interest of the entire community. Although it does not make as much money as the Mardi Gras and some of the debutante balls, this sort of party creates a very special kind of good will for the cause it espouses. One should not count the benefits of charity parties solely at the ticket office; it's an exercise in public relations as well as an effort to raise cash.

PUBLIC RELATIONS

Your third key to success in charity partygiving is as essential as organization and imagination. All the wit and good will in the world won't get you anywhere unless you can make yourself heard. Publicity is the life blood of any fund-raising party, and your publicity chairman has to know what she's doing.

Some large organizations make a big business of their parties and hire professional publicity agents, but most groups must rely on their members for this chore. Your publicity chairman should be reliable, accurate, personable and enthusiastic about the task at hand. Society editors tell me that they "could write a book" about the mistakes of volunteer press chairmen: the ones who flounce in with a boring little release and demand "a big spread" ... the ones who go over their heads to the managing editor, or even the publisher . . . the shy ones, too, who really have a story, but have no idea how to present it.

The days are rapidly disappearing when women's pages are filled with dull committee lists and pictures of ladies in little hats "planning a party." Newspapers want to present behind-the-scenes stories of real people doing things that are bright and interesting. Society editors have to entertain their readers, and they expect the publicity chairman of a charity event to provide material that's entertaining.

Here's how to organize a publicity campaign for a charity party:

1. Pick your chairman—and she'd better be good!
2. See that your chairman gets an adequate committee.
3. Send out first notice to the newspapers, or your publicity chairman may telephone or call in person. Check out the date. No use going ahead with it if the day has already been taken by a group which will appeal to the same people.
4. Announcement of party date, with name of chairman, party theme (unless it is being saved for a surprise announcement) and assisting committees.
5. Kick-off party—may come next, in cities and towns where competition for publicity has forced volunteer groups to give a small party before the big one, to get attention from the press, radio and TV. *Make this interesting!* (Fur-fashion show? Give a preview at the zoo! Industrial or office house tour? Send a Rolls with chauffeur over to the news office, and bring your editors and photographers to the Playboy Club for cocktails!)
6. The Publicity Campaign, continuing during the weeks before the party. Plan releases at regular

intervals, with *new information* each time. "Exclusives" for local columnists—inside details or gossippy news items. Dream up interesting photo possibilities, etc.

7. Party Day—publicity chairman is hostess to those who are covering the event. Sees that they get tickets, are assigned to good tables, etc. If newspaper sends cameraman without a reporter, the publicity chairman must see to it that names are correct and correctly spelled, for captions.

The lot of a publicity chairman is a hard one. If the party fails everyone is going to blame her. On the other hand, if it's a big success she is the heroine.

Each committee member will have something unique to contribute to the party if you have a good working organization. Be sure you have not only a good over-all party chairman and a smart publicity chairman, but also someone in charge of decorations who has that magic touch. Decorations are extremely important at charity parties, and here it's the big picture, painted with the broad brush, that really counts. You want people to walk into the room and say "Wow!" even if they don't remember any details afterward. Nothing dinky or fussy will do at all. You need to use spectacular techniques, with everything over scale, and you want a sense of warmth and excitement—use the hot colors—red, pink, orange and yellow. If you overdo it with the whites, blues and greens people will get a cool feeling about the party. Forget the corners of rooms at a big party. Decorators so often put trees or great arrangements of flowers in corners, but it's a waste.

Decorations that sell are a highly profitable idea. Don't waste those paper flowers and centerpieces your committee members have made by hand. People will pay good money for your cause to take these items home from the parties as mementos or as bona-fide decorations for their own homes. It is wise to remember this angle when you plan your decorating scheme. With donated materials you may be able to make some very striking objets d'art, which then can be sold for pure profit at the party's end. A recent party in San Francisco featured a number of graceful little Victorian gazebos placed around the ballroom of the Palace Hotel. A lumber company, celebrating its centennial, donated all the necessary redwood—and the gazebos were sold, before the ball took place, for $100 each!

Raffles (and other games of chance, if permitted by the law) can raise additional funds during your party. The trick is to get the items donated, publicize the donor and have a lively sales campaign before the party. When it finally takes place, have pretty girls circulate to sell as many more tickets as possible before the drawing is held.

A few more suggestions on moneymaking: programs are profitable. You'll need a committee for your program, and this group will be hard-working. Members must canvass the entire area selling ads for the magazine-style production which will be offered to buyers at the party. The usual information will be included—committee, sponsors, order of events—but the point of it, of course, is the advertising, which can add hundreds or even thousands of dollars to your profit. If socially prominent women in your organization are willing to pose for the ads, the companies are generally easily enough persuaded to invest, for prestige purposes.

And finally, don't overlook the possibility of having a sponsor or sponsors underwrite the cost of the party, so that all the money you take in will be profit. Sometimes an individual will do this (and take his contribution as an income tax deduction), or maybe a business firm hopes to create good will and increase sales as a result of this co-operation. Occasionally you will find a donor who wishes to remain anonymous; but more usually sponsors expect to be well publicized for their efforts, so there is another job for the publicity chairman.

I've done a good deal of work on benefits in various capacities, but my favorite memory is the very first big charity party I ever managed. The whole thing was so impossible from the start that I still can't quite believe it really happened. But it did—and a little orphanage far away in the Azores is $2,000 richer because of it.

I was living there with my Air Force husband, who was stationed in this unlikely spot 2,500 miles due east of Philadelphia, 700 miles west of Portugal. Right in the middle of noplace, in other words. I was stir-crazy in no time at all. For recreation there was bridge at the Officers' Club—and then, for a change of pace, there was bridge at the Officers' Club. I guess I read all the mail-order catalogues from cover to cover half a dozen times before my big idea hit me. I'd give a tremendous party, of course. It would be a benefit—a fashion show. Women on the base were starved for the sight of chic clothes, and most of them were as bored as I was. They'd love to help me with a project like this, I figured. And we'd be accomplishing something worthwhile for our hosts in the Islands, while we were at it.

There was only one little problem, or so I thought. That 2,500 miles of water between us and the nearest dress shop! I got busy writing letters. And I began talking up the fashion-show idea, which met with instant and overwhelming enthusiasm wherever I mentioned it.

I wrote to eight stores in the United States, asking if

they would be willing to ship fashions to me on consignment for my project. Rich's Department Store of Atlanta, Georgia, was the one that came through. Southern hospitality again! We drew up committees, selected models, and sent their measurements back to the States. But this couldn't be just an ordinary fashion show, I decided, with models parading up and down a makeshift runway—too much was at stake. I wanted as many people involved as possible. What we needed was a full-fledged theatrical performance, and after the show a tremendous charity ball. It would be the biggest thing that had ever happened in the Azores.

"Guys and Dolls" was the theme we chose, and the title of our party, lifted from the song in that show, was "Take Back Your Mink." I found a terrific little Portuguese combo to do the music for us, and they learned every line from the score of the Broadway production. How those wonderful people could play, too! The composer never would have recognized the results, but for sheer spirit and zest it was absolutely overwhelming.

We scouted the base for the rest of our talent. Writers, artists, decorators, carpenters, electricians, actors and actresses, models, dancers, singers and experienced committeewomen suddenly turned up on every side. Bridge games were abandoned while everyone hammered and nailed, painted, rehearsed and ran around town distributing flyers for "Take Back Your Mink." At this point someone decided that the room we were using at the Officers' Club was overdue for a remodeling job. So they took the room down right around us as we worked, and then went about putting it up again. It was to be rechristened the Lisbon Room, we were told. Meantime we were going out of our minds.

The pressure built up to a terrific pitch during the days

immediately preceding the party. Military personnel were enlisted to aid the gallant ladies in their final struggles. We were still rehearsing without the clothes from Rich's, and everyone was frantic with fear they wouldn't arrive in time. Finally the news came through—our shipment had found its way onto a nonstop flight, direct to the Island. The models dashed to the landing strip and picked up their clothes exactly two hours before curtain time! Needless to say, there wasn't time for any final fittings. But everything fit perfectly—or, at least we thought it did—with a little holding up of skirts and a clothespin here and there.

It was a beautiful show, and an unforgettable charity ball. It was one of those all-out efforts, with so many people working so hard together, month after month—and yet when this happens it still seems like a miracle. Any woman who has given her last ounce of energy to one of these tremendous productions, will know exactly how we felt. The party afterward was like a crazy dream. I'll *never* forget that wild little combo playing over and over again "Follow the Fold and Stray No More" while the entire population of the base whooped it up.

Incidentally, every single piece of clothing sent by Rich's was sold that night. It was one of the happiest moments in my life when I delivered that check for $2,000 to the little orphanage in the neighboring town. The sheer work involved in charity party-giving is tremendous, but I think the satisfactions are, very often, beyond compare.

CHAPTER TEN

Party of the Last Part

Some fine day, it happens to most of us—we fall in love, and stay that way. The Party Buddy, the Interesting Misfit, the Amiable Neuter and all the rest of our playmates suddenly seem rather dim and boring, in comparison with The Big Man Himself. If the phone rings, and somebody else wants to take us out—forget it! Like adolescents we have sudden onsets of heart disease, palsy, perspiration, spots before the eyes and other symptoms of acute distress whenever The Man appears on the scene. And like lovers through the ages we claim, and really believe, that we have never been happier in our lives! We're nuts, all of us—but long live that kind of nuttiness. If people hadn't felt this way through the centuries none of us would be around to wonder why today.

A man in love may be crazy, but a girl in love is crazy like a fox. She knows that marriage wasn't invented by The Single Man. It's up to the fox to set *this* tender trap. When she's made up her mind that this is the man she really wants, not just for a night, or a dozen nights, but for a lifetime, then it's time for her to wipe the spots from

167

her eyes, retire to her lair and do some very careful thinking. When the trap springs it's got to be entirely painless. Not only that, but he has got to think it was *his* idea—and men are not as dumb in real life as they are in storybooks.

I must say we don't get much help from the advertising image of the average American housewife these days, either. All those boring, sexless little wives in aprons, polishing floors, while the horrible, ill-mannered children come piling in, tracking mud all over the place! All that earnest conversation about vitamins, soap, kitchens and laundry! Good heavens, what a life! I can't blame any man for not wanting to get married. The girl who wants marriage has a lot to overcome. First of all she has to convince him that marriage with *her* is not going to be anything like this. And it better not be, either, if she wants to stay married. Only a TV husband would put up with it.

A real man wants a real woman and a house that is really a home. If you're beginning to think in terms of The Real Thing it's time for you to take a good look around your apartment and another look at your possessions, your clothes—and at yourself—from a new point of view. Your image as a single girl, career girl and Party Girl may well have been so chic and feminine that there's no place for an ever-loving man to stretch out and put his feet up in the entire little world you've created. You don't want him to think that where you are there is no room for him. In fact you want him to know—in time—that he is exactly what you've been waiting for.

And so, in spite of all the glamour of cocktail parties, formal dinners and charity balls, the most important party you ever give will be that intimate little dinner for two the first time you ask him to dine with you alone. This is a moment of some tension and anxiety—embarrassment, even—for many girls. No matter what the relationship has

168

been up to now, this is, fairly obviously, a bid for more serious attention. If they *haven't* been intimate, the girl is afraid that the man will think she is trying to seduce him. If they *have*, she is afraid that he will think she wants a marriage proposal. In either case, of course, what she is so afraid he may suspect is probably true. So the best cure for her jitters is to admit all to herself in privacy and to concentrate on how to make that man as comfortable and relaxed as possible during the evening ahead.

The atmosphere you create in this situation is far more important than any single detail. If you know your man fairly well you will have some individual notions of his likes and dislikes—and because you care for him you will cater to these. But there are a few general rules that apply to most men, and they are worth considering here.

It's a fact widely known, but too often ignored, I think, by girls living alone, that men want male-size comfort in a living room. This means at least one chair or deep, comfortable sofa that he can lounge in without getting a crick in his neck or being afraid that he's going to knock over some dinky little ornament of yours and spoil the Beautiful Symmetry of It All. Men don't care much for symmetry anyhow—they'd rather be comfortable. The old joke about the nagging wife trying to get her husband's easy chair out of the living room with the help of a frivolous decorator is very sad, actually. By all means make up your mind *before* you are married that you are going to have that chair in the living room and build the rest of your décor around it. Slick, hard-looking furniture may be chic, but it isn't sexy. Have soft pillows around, and the deepest plush in your rug that you can afford. Warm, bright colors—not too showy, because that's distracting from the glamour of you.

You want this man to know that you're alive. So show

him that the things you've chosen to have around you are alive, too. I don't mean keep a menagerie of pets. But I think it's very *female* to have plants growing, and bowls full of fruit, and various other natural objects in view. If you like to arrange fresh flowers do them casually—a bunch of daisies in a pottery mug says more about you as a woman than a cool, formal arrangement of hothouse carnations. In the autumn it's nice to keep a big wooden bowl of nuts, with a handsome nutcracker, on a table in the living room. At other times of year a bowl of fresh grapes—something to nibble on, from time to time—is a friendly offering. If you do have pets you mustn't make a big fuss over them. Your man is supposed to be your only pet tonight.

When he arrives make him feel casually at home from the start. Your apartment should smell divinely of some long-simmering casserole, but don't let the scent be too overpowering. Men are much more sensitive in the olfactory department than women. He should also be able to notice the scent of fresh greens and flowers, and the perfume you're wearing.

Give him something to do right away—mixing drinks, for example. Your bar table is set up, just as it would be for a small dinner party. The other arrangements, however, are a bit different for this occasion. You haven't cleared the tables of the casual accumulations of your daily life—the magazines, the books you've been reading, the portfolio of fashion designs, perhaps—the collection of old coins, thimbles, or whatnots that you can't resist—the pretty postcards you like to save. The place shouldn't look like a magpie's nest, but you do want it to look alive. This should be a room in which things *happen!* The room that kills love is the room which looks antiseptic with overcleaning and over-straightening—tense, self-conscious and neutral, like the waiting room at the dentist's.

You haven't finished all your hostess chores either as you would if it were an ordinary dinner party. Everything is prepared, and the signs of battle have been swept from the kitchen. But, quite deliberately, you've saved some little things to do after he arrives. Something in a chafing-dish needs to be stirred, perhaps—or you bring the ingredients for the salad dressing to the dining table and mix them there. Don't run to the kitchen and don't fuss around; just do some simple chore or other where he can watch you, so he can see how clever you are.

Wear something soft and pretty, nothing too low-cut or obviously sexy. You're not trying to show off your dimensions tonight. You want to be *totally* sexy, in a way that has very little to do with the amount of flesh that's bared. A long skirt or a simple and becoming hostess gown that comes down to the floor is best. You'll want to curl up gracefully after dinner on the sofa, or in his lap, maybe. Long skirts are the prettiest for this gambit, no matter how good your legs are.

If you have a fireplace, the fire is burning cozily when he arrives—you've lit it ahead of time, and have provided yourself with a nice, convenient supply of wood to add during the evening. Those long-burning artificial logs are very practical, and it needn't be noticed that they are not the real thing if you get them started before your guest arrives. They will burn nicely for hours, and if there's anything you don't want this evening it's interruptions! The phone is buried, I trust, in the closet under a pile of pillows, with the ring turned down to zero.

There's been a lot said about "conversation pieces" on the coffee table. Art, books, oddments you pick up at the import shop, that sort of thing. I think they're boring and very impersonal. Some of those art books are so big now you could put legs on them and use *them* for coffee tables. It's no fun any more, to snuggle up and look at them with somebody. By all means, you should have things around that you'll want to look at together, and talk about. But it is much smarter to have it be something personal and unique—and something that won't leave your knees paralyzed afterward. If a man is feeling sexy about a girl, he always likes to look at pictures of her in a sunsuit when she was about two years old—or maybe when she was a little bit older than that. It's handy to have an album of this sort lying around. And don't make him look at My Trip to Yosemite, either. If you have a nice picture of Grandpa and Grandma, frame it and hang it in the bathroom, along with your high school diploma, your Girl Scout Merit Awards, and other charming mementos of this sort.

Your bathroom should be interesting, by the way. He's bound to go in there sooner or later, and it's an intimate spot that tells a great deal about you. Please do not spray stuff in there that makes it smell like the Pinesy-Woodsy Deodorant Factory. Float a gardenia in a brandy glass on the back of the toilet, instead. Or steal some jasmine from your neighbor's garden and stick it in the toothbrush glass. House plants grow beautifully in the steamy atmosphere of a bathroom, and you should have some ferns or ivy there permanently, if possible, as well as cut flowers. Avoid cheap plastic bathroom accessories; it's better to save up for something fine and handsome, or do without. When your man comes to dinner be sure you haven't left a drab old bathrobe hanging on the back of the bathroom door—and don't put a black lace negligee there for the oc-

172

casion either. A huge, plushy bath sheet, spotlessly clean, is just as intriguing, and far more subtle. Books and ornaments belong in the bathroom, too. If you still think your w.c. lacks sex appeal, try framing a nice little collection of Renoir nudes and hang them at eye level, directly above the essential plumbing fixture, where they will be sure to receive the attention they deserve.

Whatever it is you are having for dinner, don't wait too long before serving it. The first martini may be the food of love, but the fourth means lullaby time, right after dinner. You want him to be happy and relaxed, but he has to be at least partially conscious if he's going to murmur that Sweet Something you want so much to hear. Which reminds me of a little story I picked up somewhere, about an incident known as the Eighteen-Orchid Blunder.

It seems that a certain young lady had designs on a man and set just such a scene as we are now describing, in order to bring him to the point of proposing marriage. He had a few quick ones to brace himself before he arrived, and she made the mistake of pouring him about five more very dry martinis before serving dinner. They had wine with their dinner, and started in on the champagne after dessert. Or maybe it was brandy—but anyhow, he fell on his knees and begged her, with tears rolling down his face, to marry him as quickly as possible. She accepted with equal fervor, and the following morning, telephoned him to confirm final details of their wedding plans. "Who?" was his reply. "What? Say, what happened last night, anyway?" The girl's remarks at this point will not bear repeating, but the reason for the name of the story is that his note of apology arrived later that day, in a yard-long box with a dozen and a half orchids the size of cabbages.

The intimate dinner-for-two, in the hands of a clever

173

woman, works very powerful magic, obviously! Just make sure the magic belongs to you and not to your gin, if you want to hear wedding bells. A nice way to cut the cocktail hour short is to bring in a little tray, after forty-five minutes or so, with two bowls of a delicious hot soup spiced with wine. This can be served at the coffee table, and you put the cocktail glasses out of sight. After soup you will move to the table-for-two you've arranged, in an intimate corner of the living room, or in front of the fireplace. A firmly built card table, draped to the floor in a pretty fabric, is exactly right for this purpose, and you will need two comfortable dining chairs. A low table, with cushions to sit on, is glamorous too, unless your man happens to be built like a basketball player, in which case I wouldn't advise it. You'll have candles on the table, of course, and this is the time to light the other candles in your room, discreetly flipping off a few light switches as you go. It's probably clear by now that I am a confirmed enemy of all electric companies! I have a great collection of pink 25-watt bulbs which I use whenever I am entertaining—with only a few brighter spots here and there, for practicality. During dinner the bright spot should be where *you* are—and you look best by candlelight.

When you plan your dinner menu, try your best for once to think like a man! Try to think like *your* man, in fact. Is he tired of eating out at restaurants? Does he travel a great deal? For heaven's sakes, then, don't give him lamb chops and baked potatoes with sour cream. Don't give him *anything* that's served at every cafeteria and airport dining room across the country! Is he the kind of man who thinks it isn't really a meal unless it's steak? Serve him steak then, by all means, and be sure to find out how he likes it cooked. Avoid any fussy, ladies'-luncheony items

174

like fruit cups, aspics and tiny cookies, or little things stuck on toothpicks. If you possibly can, serve him at least one dish—casserole, salad, soup, whatever—that he couldn't get anywhere else in the world, because you invented it. The food should be light, utterly delicious and succulent, lavish in appearance, and (apparently) quite simple in preparation. You should not go into the kitchen more than two or three times during the entire evening, and then only very briefly. When the meal is ended the dishes are quietly whisked onto a tray; you deposit the tray somewhere in the nether regions and forget about it. You should play the domestic scene very casually indeed under these circumstances. The French understand such things very well. They drink lightly before dinner because they appreciate good food so much; and at dinner they eat lightly, because they appreciate *l'amour* even more. Your dinner must be as near to perfection as you can manage, but it shouldn't take on such importance that both of you have to spend all your energy for the rest of the evening on the processes of digestion.

You've had wine with your dinner, of course, and you may want to bring on a bottle of port afterward, or a bottle of fine cognac if you can afford it. I would not advise a girl to serve champagne this particular evening, unless your man has brought you a bottle of it, nice and cold. In that case, obviously, he's asking for it. But champagne, on your initiative, would be too much like "Whoopee, I've got you now!" or "What'll it be, Bed, or the Little Church around the Corner?" Better to play it cool, and serve a nice Cabernet Sauvignon, or, if you want to get a little bit sexy about it, serve a well-decorated bottle of imported Liebfraumilch and ask him to translate the label for you.

After dinner—if you've made it this far—you'll retire to the sofa together for some serious conversation. Background music—if you haven't supplied it already—is now definitely part of the scene. The girl who has a hi-fi and a record collection may do well to ask her man what kind of music he would like to hear, or she may offer to play a new record she thinks he would particularly enjoy. The record *she* thinks he would enjoy is, of course, something sexy, though not blatantly so, and not too loud to discourage a sudden declaration of undying love on his part. If he tells her he would like to hear the U.S. Marine Band playing "Marching through Georgia", she had better retire to the powder room and reconsider her entire program.

Maybe he's just shy. If you suspect so, suggest a game of dominoes, gin rummy, checkers or chess. Corny, I know, but one game leads to another. Twentieth-century women are pretty good at getting men to proposition them, but our great-grandmothers knew a thing or three about how to get a bona-fide proposal. They asked their beaux to hold the skein while they wound up the knitting yarn. That's a lot cornier than dominoes, but it generally worked.

Great-Grandmother had another little stunt well worth considering. The buggy ride came *after* the engagement in those days, so she had to entertain a suitor in the living room by the fireside. During the day she did her quilting and mended all the socks—but when a beau came to call, out came a pretty piece of embroidery for her to work on while they talked. Usually it's better if you look a man in the eye and let him know that your attention is utterly and quite helplessly focused upon him. But while you're waiting for him to face the Moment of Truth, sometimes it's more tactful and encouraging to look the other way

176

from time to time. Particularly, it's encouraging if you happen to have a very beautiful profile.

The whole scene is one of casually glamorous domesticity. You want to give him the kind of evening he can imagine as a happy possibility *every* night. If he's been taking you out he probably knows you as the Party Girl in the party scene only. Try to show him that home life needn't be dull and dreary, either. Don't discuss vitamins. Don't discuss soap. Don't discuss *anything* too intensely at this particular point in your life. Ask his advice on some little matter from time to time, if you're stuck for conversation —and let the silences fall where they may. Into such silences diamond engagement rings often tumble.

What if you try this entire program on The Great Man three or four times in a row—and no tumble? My advice to you is, forget him. Easier said than done, I know. But if you've come to the point where you want to know what the future holds in store for you with this man, and if you've put your best foot forward over and over again, there's no sense getting it stuck permanently in that particular door. Stop your invitations, and if he's seriously interested at all he'll probably beat a track to your apartment in no time flat, and demand something nice in the way of a permanent arrangement. If he doesn't—*after all this*—who wants him?

Lest it be thought that I recommend any kind of a big phony scene here, in which the Party Girl tries to convince her chosen man that she is really Little Miss Homebody of the Twentieth Century—only to change her image again at the drop of a diamond solitaire and demand to be taken to nightspots seven nights a week, I want to make it entirely clear: I believe a wife should take *extra* pains at home, to entertain her husband as if he were her most honored guest. Dozens of books lately have urged women to keep things lively in the boudoir. I'm all for that, but I would like to add to my readers that it's just as important in the long run to help your husband feel happy and satisfied in the living room and the dining room too. When you invite a man you're serious about to your place you're declaring *your* intentions, in a way, and you ought to do your level best after marriage to keep up the promise you've implied. If you don't give your husband a carefree, candle-lit dinner fairly often, with the children tucked quietly out of the way and all your personal glamour intact, you may be sure some other woman will be only too happy to do it for him.

Much of what I've said in this book has applied specifically to the single girl who's on her own for the first time—but almost all of it could be applied just as well to the wife who wants to keep her marriage alive and interesting. Working wives, particularly, need to look to their laurels. They are sometimes either too bound up in their jobs or too tired from working to function as wives when they come home. Whether you work because you want to or because you have to, you should always remember your husband comes first. The simple reason for this is that marriage works better that way.

The harassed young woman who rushes home from work and plunges into the kitchen with a martyred air is headed for trouble. That was the way it was with Gerry, a girl I used to work with at Joseph Magnin's. She adored her husband, and she was working so he could finish law school. She was overzealous to do her part: all the cleaning, cooking and housekeeping were *her* jobs, she felt. She never asked for help and so she never got any. Her job was demanding and the hours were long; it was after six before she got home and started to cook dinner. She was always in a hurry, as if to prove how worthwhile a person she was, and how much she loved her Joe.

After several months of this Joe was completely miserable and Gerry was on the verge of a nervous breakdown from sheer exhaustion. Joe was not to blame—she was consumed with ambition to do everything, and be everything, for him. What she was forgetting in all the rush was that Joe hadn't married her in order to get himself a free live-in housekeeper. He loved Gerry just as much as she loved him. The girl he had married had been sexy and bright, glamorous, fun-loving, and full of interesting ideas. In an effort to please Joe—and in an effort, perhaps, to live up to some false idea she had of what a wife should be— Gerry was rapidly transforming herself into the kind of dull, tired nobody that Joe never would have looked at twice, to begin with.

I found Gerry in tears in her office one day, and we talked about it. She pointed to a grease spot on her skirt and said, "My God, I don't even have time to get my clothes to the cleaner's any more." and I decided we ought to begin right there. A few questions revealed that Gerry always rushed straight home and into the kitchen without bothering to change her clothes. No wonder her wardrobe problems were becoming serious! She cooked dinner against a looming deadline every night that was purely imaginary—no wonder her home life was tense and unsatisfactory for both of them! Their budget was tiny, of course, but I dragged Gerry downstairs without further delay and made her buy two $9.98 long cotton shifts, both of them colorful and very becoming to her. She promised me that she would change, from now on, every single evening as soon as she got home—and sit down with Joe in the living room for half an hour for a bit of music and conversation, and a glass of wine, before tackling her kitchen chores,

Gerry had been an indefatigable Party Girl before her marriage, and a marvelous hostess. As soon as she got back into costume, so to speak, a magical change seemed to take place in her attitude. She began to apply the same kind of inspiration and organization to her little dinners alone at home with her husband that she had formerly used in rather large-scale entertaining. A little on the compulsive side still, she started to plan menus far in advance, and began preparing most of her dishes before she left for work in the morning. Soon she discovered that Joe, who was always home much earlier than she, was delighted to put a casserole into the oven for her or simmer a stew. In time he even concocted a few dishes of his own to surprise her. Gerry was pleased and touched, and in her newly relaxed mood invited a few friends in from time to time to share their pleasant evenings. It had dawned on Joe by this time, too, that his wife would have a great deal more sparkle and zest if he did a certain amount of the heavy housework for her. It simply had not occurred to him before.

Their marriage is still a happy one, several years and three babies later. Gerry no longer works, and she is able to concentrate the full force of her talent, which is considerable, upon household management and the care of her husband and children. She still remembers to dress in something soft and feminine every evening, and she serves an intimate dinner for Joe several times each week.

I stopped by to see Gerry and Joe a short time ago, one evening during the cocktail hour. The air was chilly outside, and I made my way gratefully to their fireplace, where a fire was blazing nicely. Fresh flowers were everywhere in their living room, and I could smell something divine simmering in the kitchen. The children, freshly scrubbed, were just saying goodnight, and they drifted upstairs with sleepy yawns and giggles, as Gerry, resplendent in long black velveteen with white lace collar and cuffs, stood in the front hall blowing kisses and telling them to shoo.

"I know you're expecting guests," I said. "I'll only stay a minute."

"Not at all," said Joe. "This is just for Gerry and me. Won't you stay?"

"I can't," I replied. "I have to go home and finish that book. But tell me honestly, Joe, is it as glamorous around here as this every night? I mean, you must be kidding."

"Well, not every *single* night," said Joe. "We're having a party tonight, Gerry and I." He winked at me. "She's quite a Party Girl, you know."